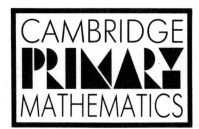

CAMBRIDGE PRIMARY MATHEMATICS

Module 5

Teacher's resource book

Roy Edwards, Mary Edwards and Alan Ward

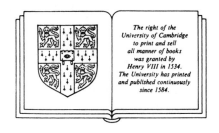

The right of the University of Cambridge to print and sell all manner of books was granted by Henry VIII in 1534. The University has printed and published continuously since 1584.

Cambridge University Press

Cambridge

New York   Port Chester   Melbourne   Sydney

Published by the Press Syndicate of the University of Cambridge
The Pitt Building, Trumpington Street, Cambridge CB2 1RP
40 West 20th Street, New York NY 10011, USA
10 Stamford Road, Oakleigh, Melbourne 3166, Australia

First published 1990
Reprinted 1991

Printed in Great Britain by Scotprint, Musselburgh

British Library cataloguing in publication data

Edwards, Roy
Cambridge primary mathematics
Module 5
Teachers resource book
1. Mathematics–For schools
I. Title   II. Edwards, Mary
III. Ward, Alan
510

ISBN 0 521 35827 2

The authors and publishers would like to thank the many schools and
individuals who have commented on draft material for this course. In
particular, they would like to thank Ronaiyn Hargreaves (Hyndburn Ethnic
Minority Support Service), John Hyland, Norma Pearce and Anita Straker,
who wrote the chapter on 'Using the computer'.

DP

CONTENTS

Mathematical content of chapters in Module 5

	Block 1		Block 2		Block 3
Number (mainly addition)	1	Addition of HTU with exchanging from tens Odd and even numbers	6	Addition of HTU with exchanging from units and tens Further place value of HTU Number patterns Strategy for adding 9	11 Place value of ThHTU Number patterns Addition of ThHTU with exchanging from units Addition of ThHTU with exchanging from tens Subtraction of ThHTU with no decomposition
Number (mainly subtraction)	2	Further subtraction of HTU with decomposition from tens Subtraction by counting on and back Problem situations	7	Subtraction of HTU with decomposition from hundreds Number patterns Strategy for subtracting 9	12 Subtraction of HTU with decomposition from hundreds and tens Place value of ThHTU Rounding numbers Addition and subtraction strategies Introduction of negative numbers
Shape	1	Use of mirror for symmetry Completing shapes Types of movement Planes of symmetry	2	Tessellating and non-tessellating shapes	3 Nets of cube and cuboid
Number (mainly multiplication)	3	Multiplication patterns for 6, 9 Multiplication of TU by 1 digit (answer in HTU) Number patterns Linking multiplication and division	8	Multiplication patterns for 7, 8 Multiplication of TU by 1 digit Multiplication by 10 Simple function machines	13 Multiplication square to 10×10 Multiplication of TU by 1 digit (all tables to 10) Factors Number patterns
Area	1	Area of irregular shapes by counting squares Use of half-square method	2	Introduction of cm^2	3 Drawing and finding areas of shapes in cm^2
Number (mainly division)	4	Division of TU by 6 and 9 Different forms of recording Division of TU by 1 digit Linking multiplication and division	9	Division of TU by 7 and 8 Division with remainders Linking multiplication and division	14 Division of HTU by 1 digit
Data	1	Bar charts (1:10 scale) Interpretation of graphs Charts to classify data Outcome of events	2	Simple co-ordinates (2, 3) notation	3 Bar-line graphs
Money	1	Addition and subtraction of £ and pence Making up amounts with coins Bills and change	2	Multiplication of pence with exchanging Linking addition and multiplication of money	3 Division of money
Number (fractions)	5	Addition of ½s and ¼s using shapes Revision of equivalent fractions ($1 = \frac{4}{4} = \frac{2}{2}, \frac{1}{2} = \frac{2}{4}$)	10	⅓ of shapes, numbers and objects	15 ⅛ of shapes and numbers Equivalence ($\frac{1}{2} = \frac{2}{4} = \frac{4}{8}$)
Length	1	Measuring in cm and m using tapes and trundle wheels Estimation	2	Perimeters of shapes	3 Notation 1 m 27 cm = 1·27 m Addition and subtraction of m and cm
Weight	1	Addition and subtraction of grams Estimating weight Weighing activities	2	Multiplication and division of grams	3 Notation 1234 g = 1·234 kg Addition and subtraction of g and kg
Volume and Capacity		**Capacity 1** Use of ml and l Addition and subtraction of ml Problem situations		**Capacity 2** Problems involving ml and litres	**Volume** Volume of shapes by counting cubes
Time	1	Minutes to/past in 5 minute intervals including digital	2	a.m. and p.m. times	3 Days in the months Calendar work Dates in words and numbers (24.11.89)
Angles	1	Four points of compass Introducing 90° and 180° Developing sense of direction	2	Eight points of compass Half right angles and 45°	3 Obtuse and acute angles Straight angles

INTRODUCTION

Aims

Cambridge Primary Mathematics is designed for 4–11 year old children. It takes into account current thinking in mathematical education and in particular it provides opportunities for:

- exposition
- discussion
- practical work
- consolidation and practice
- problem-solving
- investigational work

It is also designed to make mathematics relevant for the children and there is considerable emphasis on presenting the mathematics in real situations. Calculator work is incorporated throughout at the discretion of the teacher and ideas are given for using the computer. The materials are for children of all abilities and particular thought has been given to those with special educational needs.

Cambridge Primary Mathematics provides you with a sound foundation for all your mathematics teaching. It is *not* trying to take the place of a teacher, but rather acknowledge your professionalism. All the materials that make up Cambridge Primary Mathematics are giving you, the teacher, a core of valuable resources, so you can teach mathematics in whatever way suits you best. Cambridge Primary Mathematics can be used in its entirety and does not need additional material in order to provide a thorough mathematics curriculum. However you may prefer to teach using a variety of materials and Cambridge Primary Mathematics will give you a rich source of teaching ideas which you can supplement.

The materials

Each topic can be introduced to a class or group with activities and discussion. Ideas for these are given in the teaching notes. The children can then try the relevant chapter in the pupils' book.

Pupils' books

Each chapter in the pupils' books has its concepts developed in three stages.

Section A is intended for all children and care has been taken to make it easily accessible. It consolidates the introduction, discussion and practical work provided by the teacher and finishes with a problem or

Module	For teachers	Pupils' core materials		Reinforcement and enrichment			Assessment
1 4–5 yrs	Module 1 Teacher's resource pack	Module 1 Workbooks		Module 1 Games pack Module 1 Extra cut-up cards and rules Module 1 Rhymes pack			
2 5–6 yrs	Module 2 Teacher's resource pack	Module 2 Workcards		Module 2 Games pack Module 2 Extra cut-up cards and rules			
3 6–7 yrs	Module 3 Teacher's resource pack	Module 3 Workcards		Module 3 Games pack Module 3 Extra cut-up cards and rules			
4 7–8 yrs	Module 4 Teacher's resource book	Module 4 Book 1 Module 4 Book 2	Module 4 Answer book	Module 4 Skill support activities	Module 4 Games pack Module 4 Puzzle pack Module 4 and Module 5 Project booklets	S O F T W A R E	Module 4 Assessment pack
5 8–9 yrs	Module 5 Teacher's resource book	Module 5 Book 1 Module 5 Book 2	Module 5 Answer book	Module 5 Skill support activities	Module 5 Games pack Module 5 Puzzle pack		Module 5 Assessment pack
6 9–10 yrs	Module 6 Teacher's resource book	Module 6 Book 1 Module 6 Book 2	Module 6 Answer book	Module 6 Skill support activities	Module 6 Games pack Module 6 Puzzle pack Module 6 and Module 7 Project booklets		Module 6 Assessment pack
7 10–11 yrs	Module 7 Teacher's resource book	Module 7 Book 1 Module 7 Book 2	Module 7 Answer book	Module 7 Skill support activities	Module 7 Games pack Module 7 Puzzle pack		Module 7 Assessment pack

investigation. Children who need further reinforcement can be given work from the skill support masters.

Section B is suitable for the majority of children and covers the same concepts in more breadth, and again includes an investigation.

Section C, which includes a further investigation, can be used as extension work.

The work in these sections is usually based on a theme of interest to children (e.g. castles, the school play, etc.) in order to give the material more cohesion and to make it relevant to the environment.

This structure ensures that all children can follow a basic course of mathematics, covering all the concepts at whatever stage is appropriate to them. Organisationally this allows the teacher to teach the children as a class or in groups, as all sections cover the same topics but at increasing breadth. Children who complete only section A will not be left behind in the progression. The A, B, C format will provide for problem-solving and investigational skills to be developed across all areas of the mathematics curriculum by all children.

Logos

Throughout the pupils' books, certain logos are used to show children the items they will need or which would be particularly helpful.

shows that squared paper is needed.

 means a clock face stamp would be useful.

 tells children they can time themselves.

 indicates that a calculator would be useful.

 shows that glue is required.

 indicates that scissors are needed.

The logos are used partly to reduce the language in instructions and partly to give children visual clues for items they need.

Coloured text

Two colours of text are used in the pupils' books in order to help the children. Black text is used for instructions and information. Blue text shows the parts the children will need to record in their books.

Answer books

The answer books contain reduced facsimiles of the pages in the pupils' books. The answers are superimposed.

Games packs

There is a games pack for each module. The games are linked to the mathematical content of the course and are intended to consolidate children's skills and also to encourage children in logical thinking and development of strategies.

Puzzle packs

There is a puzzle pack for each of Modules 4–7. These packs provide extra extension material and additional interest.

Skill support activities

The packs provide extra work for those children who need it. One set consolidates the basic concepts, and another set develops the concepts still further for the more able.

Project booklets

These are written for use by pupils and provide opportunities for project work and the linking of mathematics with the environment and with other areas of the curriculum.

Software

The software is intended to develop problem-solving skills. It is not linked to any particular chapters.

Organisation and management

The materials needed are readily available, but to help you further there is a complete list of all equipment required at the end of this book. Materials can be collected, boxed and labelled so that they are easily accessible to the children. Picture labels will help those with reading problems.

Cambridge Primary Mathematics is not intended as a scheme for children to work at individually, but instead to give you control over how the mathematics is taught. The following ideas have been suggested by teachers who used the early materials.

- Introduce each topic using your own ideas plus the information in the teacher's notes.
- Let children develop the concepts at their own levels using the A, B, C structure and the skill support masters.
- Some of the investigations are particularly suitable for work and discussion in a large group or whole class.
- Overcome a shortage of equipment, like balance scales, by organising groups to work at several different activities.
- Use the games and puzzles to reinforce particular teaching points or skills as part of the normal mathematics lesson.
- Look for the calculator games in the teacher's notes.

Cambridge Primary Mathematics gives you the space to include your own ideas and to develop concepts as part of the whole curriculum.

Using the teacher's resource book

There is a section in the teacher's book for each chapter of the pupils' material. The format for each one is as follows:

Purpose

This outlines the mathematical objectives of the pupils' pages for the particular chapter.

Materials

This lists all the materials required by the pupils as they work through the mathematics.

Vocabulary

This provides you with the essential mathematical vocabulary that is used in the pupils' books. You will know which words the children will be meeting and be able to introduce them during earlier teaching sessions.

Teaching points

This section contains possible teaching approaches and activities for all the mathematics in the pupils' books. Many of these are introductory activities for the concepts. As well as activities, the notes are full of ideas and games to add to your own approach and already successful methods. You will also find ideas for mental skills, such as a quick way to add two 2-figure numbers, that will help children master and enjoy mathematics.

The Cockcroft report emphasises the importance of discussion between teacher and child, and between children. These notes give you suggestions for questions to set discussion going, and give children the opportunity to talk, ask questions and develop their mathematics. It also allows you to listen to the children and see how their understanding is developing.

There are also ideas for introducing the practical activities and further suggestions for developing these.

Using the calculator

In this part there are ideas for incorporating a calculator into mathematics. The calculator is to be used at your discretion and there will be occasions when you won't want the children to use one. However, you will probably want to have calculators readily available and there will be times when children will need a calculator to help them complete their work. The calculator is a useful aid for children to develop a particular piece of mathematics. In the pupils' book a logo is used to indicate where a calculator will be especially useful.

Links with the environment

These notes show how the mathematical ideas may be related to the everyday environment or linked to other curriculum areas. You can develop these ideas further and incorporate them into topic work across the curriculum. The project booklets will also be useful in developing many of these ideas.

Notes on investigations

Investigations are essentially open-ended situations where different approaches can be made. The notes are not meant to be used rigidly but to give guidance and suggestions for developing the mathematics. There is an additional section on investigations included in the introduction (pages 10–11).

ISSUES IN MATHEMATICS TEACHING ▰▰▰▰

Language in mathematics

Language gives mathematics context and meaning. It sets the scene, poses problems and gives information. But the way language is used and how children interpret it is crucial to their success and progress. How then does language affect mathematics?

The words used are important. Some are found only in mathematics and have to be learned, like 'parallelogram' and 'right-angle'. Some, like 'add' and 'equal', have the same meaning in or out of mathematics, and some, the ones most likely to cause problems, have different meanings according to their context; 'table' and 'difference' have both mathematical and ordinary English meanings.

Not only are the words important but so is the style of writing. There will be *explanations* of concepts, methods, vocabulary, notation and rules. *Instructions* will tell the reader what to do, and *exercises* will give practice of the skills and set problems or investigations. *Peripheral text* will introduce exercises or give clues to ways of approach, and *signals* give structure to the text with headings, letters, numbers, boxes and logos. Children must be able to see their way through all these forms of writing.

But, in addition to the words and writing, mathematics also involves reading visual information. A good mathematics text should use illustrations effectively to add information. They should not be purely for decoration, or related but not essential to the mathematics. There are also many forms of visual language which children need to understand. These include tables, graphs, diagrams, plans and maps. It is important to teach children to decode this information, interpret and make use of it, and present their answers or conclusions in different forms.

The skills children need for reading mathematics have only been touched on here. An awareness of the complexities involved will help you to overcome any difficulties caused by language and so prevent them becoming mathematical problems too. Useful books to read are *Children Reading Mathematics*, by Hilary Shuard and Andrew Rothery (John Murray) and *Maths Talk*, from The Mathematical Association.

Mathematics and special needs

Many difficulties which children experience with mathematics are not genuinely mathematical. Children with special educational needs, for whatever reasons, may have problems with mathematics because of a wide variety of factors. By looking at possible causes of difficulty many problems can be prevented or at least significantly helped.

In writing Cambridge Primary Mathematics careful attention has been given to making the mathematics accessible to *all* children, particularly in the A sections. The following areas have been looked at carefully.

Mathematical language

- Familiar words
- Words in context
- Repetition of important words and phrases
- Clear and unambiguous instructions
- Clear indication of response expected
- Sentences of a suitable length and structure
- Clear and unambiguous symbols

Presentation

- Appropriate quantity of work
- Interesting and relevant illustrations
- Variety of presentation
- Attractive page layout to encourage a positive attitude

Independence

- Clear indication of apparatus needed
- Materials that will be readily available
- Instructions children will be able to read and understand

Recording

- No unnecessary writing
- Minimum writing to help children with motor-control difficulties
- Word prompts to aid spelling

Practical work

- Plenty of practical activities
- Use of concrete apparatus encouraged
- Practical work encouraged and built in to the maths

Attitude

- Children are given a purpose to their work
- The mathematics is put in meaningful contexts
- Mathematics is related to other curriculum areas

There are some aspects of special needs that can only be dealt with by you in the classroom. For example, children may not be able to get all the equipment they need and so labelling boxes and drawers with pictures can help. Sometimes their handwriting can cause problems through poor letter or number formation, or because they are left-handed, and extra practice in this may be needed.

Skill support masters for section A give extra support and reinforcement for those children needing further practice or consolidation. Where possible, alternative methods of approach have been given but the masters are essentially to strengthen work already done.

Mathematical language, presentation, independence, recording, practical work and, just as important, the attitude children bring to their work are all vital for success. By identifying whether a difficulty is genuinely mathematical you can remove or alleviate many problems. You know your children best, and by looking at all the factors affected their learning you can meet their special needs. By doing so, you can give them the love and fascination for mathematics so that they achieve to the best of their potential.

English as a second language in mathematics

Research suggests that many children lack a firm grasp of the language of mathematics. In the case of children with English as a second language, this is often compounded by other language difficulties.

All pupils need the opportunity to hear and use the correct mathematical vocabulary. They need to develop concepts and the appropriate language together. You should not assume that because children can perform a mechanical mathematical task that they understand the associated language. You can check this by discussion with the pupil.

Practical activities are the essential starting point for any topic. Every opportunity should be taken to use correct mathematical vocabulary with pupils and to encourage them to use it when talking with other children and teachers. Where possible this vocabulary should be reinforced in other curricular areas, e.g. art and craft, games, PE etc.

Activities which offer opportunities for group work are also very useful for language development since the children are required to cooperate and to discuss the work they are doing. Investigations, calculator and computer work all lend themselves to pair or group activities.

When discussing work or activities with the children you should try to avoid the questioning approach which only requires short or one-word answers. Instead encourage full explanations of pupils' thoughts and actions using the correct vocabulary.

Weaknesses in mathematical language and the comprehension of mathematical texts often only become apparent in the junior school where greater emphasis is placed on reading and recording. Even pupils who can read a mathematical text may well be unable to interpret it. Oral discussion, individually or in groups, will help to develop the skills required.

Special attention should be given to words which sound similar; for example, 'hundred' 'hundredth', and 'seventeen' 'seventy'.

Pronunciation is often a problem with second-language learners because certain sounds may not exist in their mother tongue. However, they should be encouraged to attempt to make the distinctions clear.

Words which have a different meaning mathematically than in normal English usage – like 'similar', 'difference' and 'table' – also need special attention.

It is important not to skimp on the language aspect of mathematics in order to 'push on' with mechanical exercises and recording. A weak language base will lead to downfalls later.

Mathematics and gender

There is evidence that in the past many girls have under-achieved in mathematics. The reasons for this are complex and only an indication can be given here. Although the problem may only become apparent in the secondary school, the roots of it can often lie in the primary school.

In Cambridge Primary Mathematics there has been an attempt to produce material which will encourage girls as much as boys. As far as is possible, the pupil materials show equal numbers of girls and boys, show them participating equally in all types of activity, and illustrate how mathematics can be used in situations familiar to girls as well as to boys.

However, the written materials are only a part of the mathematics teaching. There is a great deal that you, as a teacher, can do to help the girls in your class.

- Try to encourage girls to use apparatus and toys which encourage spatial awareness, for example, Lego. Girls often have less access to this kind of toy at home, and an intuitive feeling for space is important for later work.
- Try to make sure that you spend as much time interacting with girls as with boys. It is very easy to give more time to a group of demanding boys and to leave a group of quiet girls to get on with their work.
- There has been research which shows that girls in primary schools are less likely than boys to have a calculator, to own a digital watch and to have a microcomputer at home. You may find it useful to do a survey of your class so that you are aware of the children who may need extra help with these items.

If you would like to find out more about encouraging girls to achieve their potential in mathematics, then you may find it useful to read *Girls into Mathematics* by the Open University (published by Cambridge University Press). The book was written mainly for teachers in secondary school, but many of the activities could be adapted easily for use in primary schools.

Using the calculator

Calculators are now widely available and are used extensively in the world of work. It is therefore important that children should learn to use them intelligently. The course has been written on the assumption that children have calculators available, although the extent to which they are used is left to the individual teacher.

In the pupils' books a logo is used to show activities which would particularly benefit from the use of a calculator. The teaching notes contain suggestions to develop use of the calculator including many ideas for games.

A simple four-function calculator is all that is required for the early part of this course. Ideally these should be to hand whenever children are doing mathematics and it should be natural for children to turn to them when they are needed. Children with special needs may need to use a calculator to complete section A even in places where the logo is not shown.

The use of the calculator has brought about a shift in the content of the mathematics included in the course. There is less emphasis on straight computation and more on problem-solving. It is also important that children develop mental strategies so that they can check that calculator answers are approximately correct and they have not miskeyed. Ideas for developing these mental skills are given in the teaching notes.

Using the computer

The computer is a useful tool for developing mathematical ideas. It can also be a useful way to get children to discuss their mathematics.

Make the most of any opportunities you have for using the computer during mathematics. Children should work at it in twos or threes as this allows scope for discussion. It is important that within each group, there is no one child dominating and restricting the participation of the others. For this reason it may be necessary to select the groups carefully.

Ideas for using the computer with Module 5 are given in the chapter on using the computer on pages 12–26. This chapter was written by Anita Straker who has a lot of experience in this area. The ideas are not restricted to any particular model of computer.

There is software planned for use alongside the course. The aim of it is to develop problem-solving skills. It is not tied to any particular chapters of the course.

Investigations

Investigations are essentially open-ended activities where children may devise various approaches. They provide an ideal opportunity for children to devise their own pieces of mathematics, to use logical reasoning, and to discuss mathematics between themselves.

Ideally children should work on investigations in small groups. This gives them the chance to talk, think and express their ideas. When they have worked on an investigation as a group for a while, it can be very beneficial to have the group report to the rest of the class on how they approached the task. This gives an opportunity for the class to see alternative approaches and various problem-solving techniques.

It is important not to make remarks that judge children's contributions and not to become so involved that the investigation ceases to be the child's. The ideal contribution from the teacher is questions such as:

> 'Why did this work?'
> 'Will it work with other shapes or numbers?'
> 'What would happen if . . .?'

The teaching notes include comments on the investigations. These are not meant to be used rigidly but merely to give some indication of where the investigation might lead. Other approaches may be just as good, or better! Children should be encouraged to find their own way of recording and to ask further questions in order to extend their work.

Algorithms

Algorithms are methods for doing calculations. On the whole, these detailed methods are not given in the texts in order to allow freedom of choice. You can introduce your preferred method, or alternatively the children can devise their own. If children do work out their own algorithms then a teaching approach similar to investigations can be used with children sharing their ideas. This approach has the advantage that the method becomes the child's own and they are more likely to remember it.

Use of practical work

Children should be encouraged to use apparatus and concrete materials whenever possible. It is important that children have plenty of experience in practical situations before moving on to doing more abstract activities. They should not be hurried into making this step.

The materials required for this course are widely available. A checklist of what you will need for Module 5 is given at the end of the book.

USING THE COMPUTER

The computer's contribution to children's mathematical work comes through using:

- specific programs in which children can explore mathematical ideas
- adventure games and simulations which support mathematics across the curriculum
- software tools like databases and programming languages which support open-ended problem-solving

In each case, the software can act as a stimulus to children to talk about mathematical ideas. Through their informal discussion with each other and with their teacher children can build sound intuitive ideas about mathematical concepts. Children need to work in small groups at the computer, so that they have a chance to share and to talk about what is happening on the screen.

Specific programs

Although there are many 'drill and practice' mathematics programs, there seems little point in using the computer for practice when there is already an abundance of mathematics practice material in books, on workcards and on worksheets.

Some of the most attractive of the specific programs are in the form of strategic games or puzzles. In these the children need to focus on the strategy which is to be used, and they will often use mental skills in the process. It is important that teachers link the use of these programs to the children's work away from the keyboard: both preliminary and follow-up activities need to be planned in advance.

There are also specific programs which encourage mathematical investigation. The starting point of the investigation should be through practical work away from the computer, but when the diagrams become too complicated, or the calculations too difficult, the computer program can take over.

Adventure games and simulations

Adventure games, based on fantasy, and simulations, based on fact, give children opportunities to solve problems across the curriculum in a context of fact or fantasy. Simulations like *Cars in Motion* (Cambridge Software House), *Suburban Fox* (Newman College) or *Bike Ride* (Energy Pack, Cambridge University Press) require strategic thinking and planning, and the use of a range of mathematical and other skills.

Adventure games, like *The Lost Frog* (ESM), *Dread Dragon Droom* (RESOURCE), *Puff* or *Martello* (A. Straker), all have a series of mathematical puzzles and problems which need to be resolved.

Primary children often lack confidence in problem-solving situations but such programs can provide them with additional opportunities for developing their mathematical thinking and increasing their range of problem-solving strategies. The role of the teacher in encouraging discussion about the possible forms of solution is an important one here. Questions like 'What would happen if instead . . .?', or 'How many different ways could we . . .?', or 'Would it be possible to . . .?', all help to extend the children's thinking about a particular problem.

Databases

Databases support a range of statistical work across the curriculum. Databases can be used to encourage the children to ask questions, to collect, organise and analyse data, and to find patterns and relationships.

There are two kinds of databases which are useful.

Sorting Game (MESU), *Seek* (Longman) and *Branch* (MEP Project Work Pack) are databases based upon a branching-tree structure. They encourage the use of very precise mathematical description in sorting and classifying. Children can set up binary-tree classification systems, using the program alongside the practical sorting activities which take place throughout the primary school.

Databases like *Our Facts* (MESU) or *Factfile* (CUP) work in the same way as a card index system. Graph drawing packages like *Picfile* (CUP), which display the data graphically, are very helpful here.

Programming

Young children begin 'to program' as soon as they start to find ways of recording things like a sequence of moves in a game, the commands to give to a battery-driven robot, or the shapes which are needed to make up a picture. A computer program, like a sheet of music or a knitting pattern, is simply a set of precise, coded instructions arranged in an appropriate order, and programming is another way in which children can use the computer as a tool to explore mathematical ideas.

The programming language which is most often used in primary schools is Logo. The point of introducing young children to programming with Logo is to allow them to feel in control, to give them a way of clarifying their ideas, and to encourage them to order their thoughts logically. Although the children will need to be taught some simple programming techniques, the emphasis needs to be not on learning these techniques, but on the mathematics that can be explored through programming.

Number

Place value

One of the most important of the mathematical concepts to be developed at this stage is the idea of place value for whole numbers. Activities with concrete materials like Dienes blocks or a number line, and activities with calculators, can be supplemented by the use of computer games. At the end of a game it is important to talk to the children about the strategies that they used. Ask them 'How did you know what to do?' or 'Did you find any quick ways of winning?'

- *Playing with Places* (Shiva – ESM): place value games for tens and units.
- *Guess* (MicroSMILE): guess a number between 1 and 1000 using clues of 'too big' or 'too small'.
- *Boxes 1, 2, 3, 4* (Number games – A. Straker): a set of four different games in which digits generated by a die must be placed in boxes representing two-, three- or four-digit numbers.
- *Minimax* (MicroSMILE): put five numbers in boxes, do a sum, and make a smaller or bigger number than the computer.

Mental strategies

There are many different computer games and puzzles that help children to develop mental strategies for dealing with numbers. Some encourage the use of addition and/or subtraction:

- *Make 57* (Number games – A. Straker): by moving around a square grid of nine numbers, the players accumulate numbers towards a total of 57.
- *Conceal* (Mathematical Games and Activities – Capital Media): roll numbers on a 1–9 die and leave the smallest totals remaining.
- *Number Puzzler* (Shiva – ESM): five number games involving logic and strategy help either one or two players to reinforce their addition and subtraction skills.

Other programs provide a motivating setting in which the recall of multiplication tables and the related division facts can be practised.

- *Gusinter* (Mathematical Games and Activities – Capital Media): two teams of players aim to cover multiples of numbers rolled on a die. The winning team is the first to get four multiples in a row.
- *Table Adventures* (Shiva – ESM): four stimulating games that help children to understand their tables through factorisation introducing prime numbers and common factors.

One possible follow-up activity to the use of strategic number games and puzzles is to suggest that the children make changes either to the numbers or to the rules and devise their own game or puzzle using card, dice and other apparatus.

Number patterns

The use of computer software to support number work can provide opportunities to explore number patterns. Although discovery of a pattern is a first step, children need to be encouraged to do more than this. Patterns can help to identify or to explain relationships, to make predictions or to form generalisations. Some of the number pattern programs may have been used at earlier stages, but options within them can offer a greater degree of challenge to the children. They require the children first to spot a pattern, and then to make use of it in some way.

- *Ergo* (MEP Microprimer): patterns in a set of two-digit numbers hidden on a square grid must be discovered with the help of clues saying 'too big' or 'too small'.
- *Monty* (ATM): the python called Monty wriggles around on a number grid. The challenge is to discover which numbers he is covering.
- *Counter* (ATM): set a starting number, and a jump size, so that patterns of digits can be explored.
- *Patterns 1* (MEP Primary Mathematics Pack – RESOURCE): choose the width of a grid and investigate the patterns created by one or two multiples.

Programs like *Counter* and *Patterns 1* are open ended – small tools which carry out particular tasks. It is up to the users to decide how to use them. For this reason, it can be helpful for the teacher to work with the children at the computer, to help them to select and refine suitable ideas. For example, with *Counter* you could decide to start on 2, and jump on in 4s.

- What is the pattern in the sequence of the units digits? How many digits are there in the pattern? Can you explain this?
- What would the sequence be if you jumped on in 14s instead? Why? Will 228 be in the pattern of 14s? How do you know?

With *Patterns 1*, you could create the pattern of fours on a grid with seven columns.

- Would 108 be in the pattern? How do you know?
- What number would be at the top of the column with 157 in it?
- What other numbers of columns would produce the same pattern for multiples of 4? What do all these grids have in common?
- What would the pattern of fours look like for a grid with five columns? Can you explain why?

Investigation

Some computer programs provide particular situations for investigation. By making generalisations about the patterns which they see, or about the relationships which they discover, the children make a gentle start to algebra. It is important to begin the investigation away from the computer using pencil and paper or other apparatus. Encourage the children to predict what will happen before they try something out. Help them to organise in a sensible way the results that they gather and to look for patterns that might help them. When diagrams become too difficult to draw, or when the numbers become too difficult to calculate, move to the computer program. At the end of the investigation, ask the children to tell you in their own words what they have found out.

- *Tiles 2* and *Tiles 3* (Mathematical Investigations – Capital Media): red and blue tiles are set out in particular arrangements; the object is to discover the relationship between the number of red tiles and the number of blue tiles.
- *Lines* (Mathematical Investigations – Capital Media): discover how many lines join the dots in one row to the dots in another row.
- *Circle* (MicroSMILE): jump round points on a circle and discover the kind of patterns produced.
- *Pattern 2* (MEP Primary Maths – RESOURCE): investigate the patterns to be found on a triangular grid.

Adventure games

For many children, one of the most exciting possibilities for using the computer is to play a mathematical adventure game in which different puzzles and problems need to be solved. Adventure games offer opportunities for cross-curricular work, since they stimulate many different activities away from the keyboard. Games like these are best played by small groups, so that discussion about strategies can take place. The children will need to keep careful records of their position in the game, the routes they follow, and the decisions they make.

Some mathematical adventure games provide a series of puzzles and problems in which the number skills developed throughout Module 5 can be applied. These are:

- *Sing a Song of Sixpence* (Yorkshire Bank – RESOURCE): this simple adventure game helps children to develop an understanding of how they can use banks and what benefits they can gain by doing so.
- *Puff* (A. Straker): the object is to find Puff the dragon and provide him with his favourite food. The program can link very readily to topic work on China and its culture.

Programming

The activities which children have been doing with their calculators can also be done with a computer. By programming the computer, using either Logo or BASIC, the children can explore the effects of typing in some simple statements to see the result on the screen. For example,

```
PRINT 36 + 49
PRINT 48 * 5 − 20/2
```

Repeated operations can also be explored and compared. The advantage of using the computer rather than the calculator is that the entire sequence of operations remains on the screen for counting and comparison. For example,

```
PRINT 5 + 5 + 5 + 5
PRINT 4 * 5
PRINT 4 + 4 + 4 + 4 + 4
PRINT 5 * 4
```

Relationships between operations can be highlighted by asking the children to type in a calculation like

```
PRINT 36 + 47   or   PRINT 56 * 6
```

and then to predict what result they will get if they type

```
PRINT 83 − 36   or   PRINT 336/6
PRINT 83 − 47        PRINT 336/56
```

Using the PRINT command, the children can try to solve some problems. For example,

- Which pairs of two-digit whole numbers give the result of 2 when one of the numbers is divided by the other?
- 159 is the sum of two consecutive numbers. What are they?
- By adding fours and fives I can make 22.
  PRINT 4 + 5 + 4 + 4 + 5
- Can I add fours and fives to make 39? What about making 110? How many different ways are there of making 60?

Children who are particularly confident with programming, may have met the idea of a **variable**, the use of a letter or word to stand in the place of a number. For example, in Logo the procedure to draw the step of a staircase could be written as

```
TO STEP
    FORWARD 30
    RIGHT 90
    FORWARD 30
    LEFT 90
END
```

When the procedure name STEP is typed, a step with a rise and tread of length 30 units is drawn. To draw steps of any size a variable must be introduced.

```
TO STEP: size
    FORWARD: size
    RIGHT 90
    FORWARD: size
    LEFT 90
END
```

When the procedure name is typed it must now be followed by a number to indicate the size of the step. STEP 50 will draw a larger step with a rise and tread of 50 units, whereas STEP 10 will draw a smaller step of size 10 units.

Variables are also useful in procedures which can be used to investigate numbers. For example, children may be building up the three times table by printing multiples of 3:

PRINT 3 * 1, PRINT 3 * 2, PRINT 3 * 3, PRINT 3 * 4, . . .

and so on. A procedure called, say, TIMES, can be written so that it has a variable input:

TO TIMES: number
    PRINT 3 * : number
END

By typing TIMES 1, TIMES 2, TIMES 3, TIMES 4, and so on, the first few multiples of 3 can be printed. Other multiples of 3 can be calculated by giving the procedure any desired input: TIMES 32, TIMES 351, TIMES 2.5, and so on. By changing the 3 in the procedure to 2, or 5, or 10, multiples of these numbers can be calculated instead. The TIMES procedure can be used to investigate questions such as 'Is 345 a multiple of 3?'

Data

Coordinates and programming

There are a number of computer programs that require the children to make use of coordinates as part of a game or puzzle. Some of these programs are computerised versions of well-known board games such as 3D noughts and crosses, or Othello. In the computer version the players need to use coordinates to tell the computer where they want to place a marker. Other programs offer alternative activities.

- *Co-ordinate Jigsaw* (Maths with a story 1 – BBC Publications): create a jigsaw by specifying the coordinates of the puzzle pieces to be changed over.
- *Pirate Gold* (Maths with a story 2 – BBC Publications): the aim is to fill a treasure chest with gold by hunting for it on an island or under the sea.
- *Lines* (MicroSMILE): play four in a row on a 9 × 9 board.
- *Rhino* (MicroSMILE): hunt a lost rhinoceros on a × 10 coordinate grid making use of clues which give the distances along the grid lines.
- *Locate* (MicroSMILE): a small cross appears within a large blank square. The object is to locate the cross by typing in two numbers to represent coordinates.

It is also possible for children to produce line drawings based on coordinates by programming the computer in either Logo or BASIC.

In **Logo**, the command to move the turtle to position (X, Y) on the screen is

SETPOS [X Y]

If the pen is up, the turtle will move to the position (X, Y) without drawing a line. If the pen is down, the turtle draws a line as it moves. The mid point of the screen is the position (0, 0). Points on the X line to the left of the centre point are negative with a minus sign; points on the Y line below the centre point are also negative. You could try experimenting with this set of commands.

SETPOS [100 300]
SETPOS [−100 300]
SETPOS [−100 − 300]
SETPOS [100 − 300]

If you are not sure about the position of the turtle on the screen, then typing

PRINT POS

will produce the coordinate position for you.

One game that children enjoy programming for each other starts by one group drawing a small square somewhere on the screen. The turtle is returned to the centre position. Then the next group tries to move the turtle into the square by using the smallest number of SETPOS commands.

Similar ideas can be developed using **BBC BASIC**, available for the RML Nimbus as well as for BBC machines, although in BBC BASIC the position (0, 0) is generally the bottom left-hand corner of the screen. Before you begin you must make sure that the screen is ready for drawing. You can do this by typing MODE 1. This command will clear the screen and place the 'pen' in the bottom left-hand corner.

There are two commands which are particularly useful to use.

MOVE 100,300

This makes the 'pen' move to the coordinate position (100,300) without drawing a line.

DRAW 300,500

This draws a straight line from the existing position to the new position of (300,500).

The diagram below shows a BASIC program which draws a house. The lines of the program have been numbered so that they correspond to the points of the drawing. You could try typing the program into your computer. When you are ready to make the program work, type

MODE 1
RUN

Housing program in BASIC

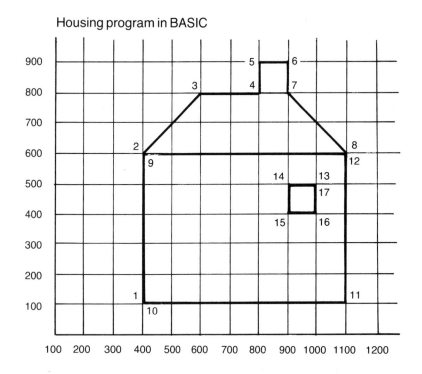

```
 1  MOVE 400,100
 2  DRAW 400,600
 3  DRAW 600,800
 4  DRAW 800,800
 5  DRAW 800,900
 6  DRAW 900,900
 7  DRAW 900,800
 8  DRAW 1100,600
 9  DRAW 400,600
10  MOVE 400,100
11  DRAW 1100,100
12  DRAW 1100,600
13  MOVE 1000,500
14  DRAW 900,500
15  DRAW 900,400
16  DRAW 1000,400
17  DRAW 1000,500
```

If you have made a mistake, the house will look rather strange! To correct the 'bug' in your program, you must first examine the instructions which you have typed. To do this, type the word

LIST

so that the lines of the program appear again on the screen. To make the correction, you do not need to type the whole program again, only the line in which the mistake appears. For example, if the mistake is in line 10, then type the whole of line 10 again, including the line number. If you then type LIST once more, then you will see that the new line 10 has replaced the old one. Try out the revised program by typing

MODE 1
RUN

Whether they are programming in Logo or in BASIC, encourage the children to suggest their own ideas for drawing. Provide them with squared paper on which to make their plans before they go to work at the computer.

Graphs, charts and tables

The computer is capable of producing a wide variety of graphs, charts and tables very quickly and accurately. It makes it possible for children to spend much more of their time on the important skills of handling real information collected by themselves, rather than merely drawing graphs related to information provided by others. It encourages the development of the following information handling skills:

- Deciding what the purpose is.
- Deciding what data to collect.
- Deciding how to collect it.
- Deciding how to record or represent it.
- Framing questions, and using the data to find answers.
- Explaining results.
- Communicating findings.

There is an easy-to-use program which children can use to display and print the data they have collected.

- *Datashow* (MEP Primary Maths – RESOURCE): a group of children, or a teacher working with them, can enter up to eight items of data, sort the items either numerically or alphabetically, and display the data in a table, bar chart or pie chart.

The program is most suitable for displaying counts of various kinds, perhaps made by a whole class, or even the whole school. Sometimes the data can be collected very quickly on a 'hands up who . . .' basis. Sometimes a group of children can conduct a survey using a simple data collection sheet.

Weights of children	Number
18 – 20 kg	/
21 – 23 kg	//
24 – 26 kg	////
27 – 29 kg	ⅢⅢ
30 – 32 kg	////
33 – 35 kg	/

A title describing what the count is about needs to be given when the data is first entered into the program. Some suggestions are:

Journey to school
walk, bus, train, tube, bike, car

Birthday season
spring, summer, autumn, winter

We can swim
5 metres, 10 metres, 20 metres, 100 metres

Ages of children
5, 6, 7, 8, 9, 10, 11

Brothers and sisters
0, 1, 2, 3, 4, 5, . . .

Wind direction
N, NE, E, SE, S, SW, W, NW

We ran 50 metres in
10–12 sec, 13–15 sec, 16–18 sec, . . .

Three times table
$1 \times 3, 2 \times 3, 3 \times 3, 4 \times 3, 5 \times 3, 6 \times 3, 7 \times 3, 8 \times 3$

After each display using Datashow, it is important to ask the children 'What does the graph show us or tell us?' and 'Why do you think that it . . . ?' If it is appropriate, ask them to place outcomes or events in order of 'likeliness' and to talk about the 'chance' of something happening. Encourage them to use words like 'unlikely', 'possible', 'likely', 'highly likely', 'highly probable' and to associate these words on a scale from 'impossible' to 'certain'.

Two times table

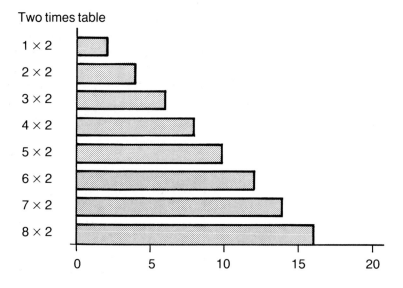

Weather in June

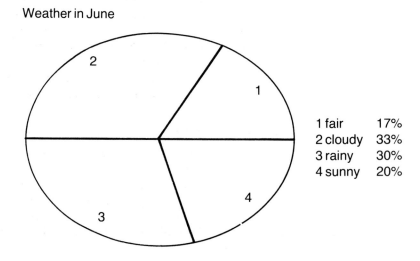

1 fair	17%
2 cloudy	33%
3 rainy	30%
4 sunny	20%

Database

Another way of using the computer to handle and display information is by using a database.

- *Ourfacts* (MESU): an introductory database which is extremely easy to use. It displays information in tables, on Venn diagrams, in pictograms, block graphs, pie charts and scattergrams. Depending on the data being collected, it can handle about 60–80 records.
- *Grass* (Newman College): a more sophisticated database which can handle much larger amounts of information. It displays information in pie charts, count graphs and scattergrams.

A database can support any cross-curricular work in which children are gathering and using information. For example, if the children are making a study of clothing, they might want to examine the coats they wear to school and look for connections between the length of the coat and its thickness, or between the length of the coat and the buttons on it. They might ask questions about the proportion of coats that have hoods or linings. Each child in the class can collect information about his or her own coat. For example,

Name:	name of child
Coat type:	anorak, coat, jacket, mac
Colour:	colour of the coat
Length:	length in centimetres
Buttons:	number of buttons
Fibre:	wool, cotton, polyester, nylon, etc
Thickness:	thick, thin, medium
Lining:	yes, no
Hood:	yes, no

Alternatively, children who are making a study of local history may be examining those gravestones in their local churchyard which relate to a particular period. The information on the gravestones may help them to answer questions on how long people tended to live, whether men or women lived longer, or what proportion of the deaths were children under the age of sixteen. They may make deductions about the customary shapes of the gravestones or the most common material from which they were made. The record for the database could look like this.

Name:	name on the gravestone
Sex:	male, female
Age:	age at death
Year:	year of death e.g. 1881
Shape:	cross, slab, tomb, etc.
Material:	granite, marble, limestone, other

When the children are making interpretations from the graphs and charts which they produce, encourage them to use familiar fractions to make estimates of proportions. When examining pie charts, for example, it is relatively easy to see things like 'about one quarter of the gravestones belonged to children' or 'about three quarters of the gravestones were slabs'. Ask them to suggest reasons for their findings. For example, it is possible that there were more child deaths because health care was less effective, or more slabs because they were cheaper to make.

Angle

Measure of turn

Children who have been accustomed to working with Logo should by this stage have a firm grasp of angle as a measure of turn. They will be comfortable with the use of degrees as a unit of measurement, although they may not be familiar with the word 'degrees' itself. They will be aware that a turn of 90 is needed to make the corner of a square, but they may not know the term 'right-angle'. They will have used commands like RIGHT 180 or LEFT 180 to make the turtle turn and face the opposite direction without necessarily talking about the turtle turning 'through a straight line'.

These new terms, as well as words like 'acute' and 'obtuse', can be introduced as children discuss their Logo drawings. 'Here the turtle turned LEFT 90 so it turned through a right-angle. Where else did you make the turtle turn through a right-angle? Where did it turn through a straight line or straight angle?'

Compass directions

You can also make use of Logo to give children a feel for compass directions. To do this you will need to make use of a Logo command which sets the turtle's heading, or the direction in which it is pointing. If you set the heading, and then type FORWARD 100, the turtle will set off in the direction of its heading. The turtle measures its heading using bearings which are measured clockwise from the top of the screen. A heading of 0 is straight up the screen, a heading of 90 is to the right, 180 is straight down, and 270 is to the left.

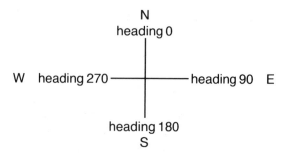

Try typing a sequence of commands using the abbreviation SETH to set the heading and FD to move forward: for example,

SETH 90   FD 50   SETH 135   FD 50   SETH 90   FD 50

You could type in four procedures for children to use. Call these procedures NORTH, SOUTH, EAST and WEST, or if you prefer N, S, E and W. The procedures are:

TO NORTH	TO SOUTH	TO EAST	TO WEST
SETH 0	SETH 180	SETH 90	SETH 270
FD 10	FD 10	FD 10	FD 10
END	END	END	END

When you have finished, the children can try tracing a path by using compass directions. They will enjoy planning 'walks' for the turtle in this way. They need only type a command like EAST, and the turtle will take a tiny step forward in an easterly direction. It is easy to add four further procedures for NW, NE, SW and SE when the children are ready to use these as well.

Adventure games sometimes offer the opportunity to use compass directions. A program which accompanies *The Lost Frog* (ESM) allows the children to create and play their own adventure using directions of north, south, east and west. There are several other computer programs which can help to give the children a feel for directions.

- *3D Maze* (MicroSMILE): the screen shows a three-dimensional view of a maze. The object is to get out of the maze. If you need help a map is displayed.
- *Pirates* (Micros in the primary classroom – Longman): find the treasure by hunting for it by making use of clues which refer to compass directions.
- *Goldhunt* (MicroSMILE): the user is taken on a seven-stage journey which must be completed by using compass directions. There are several levels of difficulty; at the harder levels the north line is unlikely to point to the top of the map!

Shape

Tessellation

Computer software can provide opportunities for building shapes and patterns, and for discovering the relationships which allow one shape to be fitted against another in a tessellation.

- *Mosaics*/BBC or *Paint*/480Z (MEP Infant pack – MESU): mosaic patterns made from squares of varying sizes can be designed and printed.
- *Picture Maker Plus* (ESM): patterns can be built up using eight colours, five shapes, and four movements, then printed out.
- *Tile Stretch* (Maths with a story 2 – BBC Publications): players take turns to fit square tiles on a board. Tiles can be stretched by a factor of 1, 2 or 3 along either the length or the breadth of the tile.

- *Tiles* (MicroSMILE): the screen displays a 10 × 7 array of square tiles. The tiles may be rotated through 90 degrees individually, or in lines (horizontal, vertical, diagonal), to make interesting patterns.

Using programs like these the children could try to fill the screen with square, rectangles, patterns of zig-zag lines, squares within squares, other shapes of their own choosing. The children can also try these same challenges using Logo, first drawing the shape of their tile and then trying to repeat it to fill the screen.

It is important to discuss with the children the properties of shapes which fit together without leaving any spaces. Why will four squares fit together round a point? When an area is covered with squares of the same size, why do these create an effect of straight lines?

Symmetry

The computer can also be used to explore line or mirror symmetry. The children can try to make symmetrical pictures or patterns with the same tiling programs that they have used to investigate space filling with simple tessellations. This time they could try to make butterflies, trees, houses on river banks reflected in the water, and so on. Other programs which can be helpful are:

- *Turnflex* (Maths with a story 2 – BBC Publications): this is a puzzle in which the aim is to rebuild a picture using mirrors and rotations.
- *Symmetry Patterns* (Maths with a story 1 – BBC Publications): this program allows children to create patterns using different kinds of symmetry, with one, two or four mirror lines.

Symmetry can also be investigated using Logo. For example, this procedure will draw a squiggle of lines on the right-hand side of the screen.

```
TO SQUIGGLE
    FD 100
    RT 90
    FD 250
    RT 90
    FD 400
    RT 90
    FD 100
END
```

What procedure would draw the reflection of the squiggle in a vertical line down the centre of the screen?

TEACHING NOTES

Number 1

Purpose

- To introduce odd numbers, even numbers and patterns for addition
- To introduce addition of hundreds, tens and units with 'carrying' from the tens

Materials

Structural apparatus, 100 square, squared paper

Vocabulary

Odd, even, middle, add, pairs, largest, smallest, sums, pattern, forwards, backwards, palindrome, squares

TEACHING POINTS

1 Odd numbers

Talk with the children about odd numbers. Explain that odd numbers end in 1, 3, 5, 7 and 9. Write the sequence of numbers 1, 3, 5, 7, 9, 11, 13, 15, 17, 19, 21, 23, 25, 27, 29 and ask
'What is the third odd number?'
'What is the fifth odd number after 17?'
   Ask them to predict the next few numbers in the pattern. Talk about their predictions. Ask such questions as
'What is the second odd number after 100?'

2 Even numbers

Talk about even numbers. Use the pattern 2, 4, 6, 8, 10, 12, 14, 16, 18, 20, 22, 24, . . . and explain that they are all even numbers because they end in 2, 4, 6, 8 and 0.
   Ask the children to predict the next few numbers in the pattern. Talk about their predictions.

3 Patterns

Talk about patterns of odd and even numbers like:

1	3	5	7	9		2	4	6	8	10
11	13	15	17	19		12	14	16	18	20
21	23	25	27	29		22	24	26	28	30

Ask the children to write the numbers 1 to 50 in different ways on squared paper and mark or colour the odd and even numbers.

1	2	3	4	5	6	7	8	9	10
11	12	13	14	15	16	17	18	19	20
21	22	23	24	25	26	27	28	29	30
31	32	33	34	35	36	37	38	39	40
41	42	43	44	45	46	47	48	49	50

1	6	11	16	21	26	31	36	41	46
2	7	12	17	22	27	32	37	42	47
3	8	13	18	23	28	33	38	43	48
4	9	14	19	24	29	34	39	44	49
5	10	15	20	25	30	35	40	45	50

1	2	3	4	5	6	7	8	9	10
20	19	18	17	16	15	14	13	12	11
21	22	23	24	25	26	27	28	29	30
40	39	38	37	36	35	34	33	32	31
41	42	43	44	45	46	47	48	49	50

Talk about the different patterns made.

4 Games to play

ODDS AND EVENS

Children play in pairs. In each pair, one child is 'odds', the other 'evens'. They throw two 1–6 dice and add the numbers. If the sum of the two numbers is odd the 'odds' player scores 1 point, if it is even the 'evens' player scores 1 point. The winner is the first to reach 10 points.

This could be played by two small teams, each team member in turn adding the numbers.

Variations could be to subtract the two numbers, or to use three dice and add the numbers. Children can make up their own variations of this game.

THE ODD/EVEN RACE

Children play in pairs with one child as 'odds' and the other as 'evens'. They take turns to throw two 1–6 dice and 'odds' tries to make an odd number while 'evens' attempts to make an even number by putting the numbers together. For example, a throw of 4, 1 could make 14 (even) or 41 (odd). One point is scored for each successful combination. Players can only score points on their own throw. The winner is the first to score 10 points.

MAKE THE NUMBERS

Divide the children into groups of three or four players. Each game requires one HTU board, two sets of cards numbered 0–9 and some target cards.

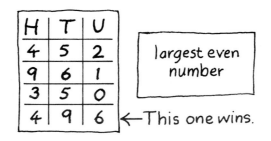

Shuffle the number cards and place them face downwards. Turn over the top target card which could be 'the largest even number', 'the smallest odd number', 'the nearest to 215', etc. Players take turns to turn over the top number card and place it on their row on the HTU board. Once placed, a number cannot be moved. When the board is complete the game is over. The winner is the player whose three-digit number satisfies the target.

H	T	U	
4	5	2	
9	6	1	largest even number
3	5	0	
4	9	6	←This one wins.

5 HTU addition

Use structural apparatus to show addition with 'carrying' from the tens. It is important to give children the imagery for this.

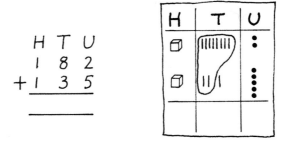

```
  H T U
  1 8 2
+ 1 3 5
_____
```

Use your usual form of words and method for recording.

Remind the children of the horizontal to vertical method of recording. Talk about whether the numbers and answers are odd or even.

```
              H T U
257 + 162     2 5 7  odd
            + 1 6 2  even
            _____
```

6 Mental work

Ask the children odd and even number problems. For example,
'Is there an odd or even number of girls in the classroom?'

Give the children practice in adding on tens mentally. For example,
162 + 10, 178 + 40, 128 + 40.

Ask the children to add numbers such as 22 + 37. Talk to them about splitting up the numbers and adding up the parts separately. for example,

$$22 + 37 = 20 + 2 + 30 + 7 \quad \text{or} \quad 34 + 29 = 34 + 30 - 1$$
$$= 50 + 9 \qquad\qquad\qquad = 64 - 1$$
$$= 59 \qquad\qquad\qquad\quad = 63$$

USING THE CALCULATOR

Remember – calculators vary in the way they work.

1 Estimation and number patterns

Revise how to switch on the calculator and enter three-digit numbers.

Let the children practise sums such as 183 + 132. Talk about the importance of estimating the answer to check the calculator result. For example, an answer of 1562 to 134 + 293 is obviously wrong since 293 is nearly 300, so the answer should be four hundred and something.

Use the constant function to add several tens, to reinforce addition of tens, place value and addition patterns. For example, 156, 166, 176, 186, 196, 206, 216, etc.

A game to play

TENS

Two players use one calculator. The first player writes two three-digit numbers which differ in the tens column only. For example, 213, 293.

The second player enters the smaller number and has to make the larger one in one addition (by adding 10 or 20 or 30 etc.). The players then change over. They have ten turns each.

The winner is the person to do it correctly the most times.

2 Odd and even

Talk about the odd and even numbers on the calculator keyboard. Let the children investigate what happens when they use odd and even numbers for addition (i.e. odd + odd, odd + even, even + odd, even + even).

LINKS WITH THE ENVIRONMENT

- Ask the children to look for odd and even numbers on the way to school. For example, house numbers are usually odd on one side of the street and even on the other.

- The pages of a book or newspaper usually have odd numbers on the right-hand page and even on the left-hand page.
- Ask the children to look for other odd and even numbers such as car numbers, sign-posts (distances), bus numbers, timetables, or packet sizes. Make a display of all the different numbers collected.

NOTES ON INVESTIGATIONS

Section A

Do the children use a system to find all the odd numbers (and later even numbers) which add up to 20?

For example

$19 + 1 = 20$	or	$1 + 19 = 20$
$17 + 3 = 20$		$3 + 17 = 20$
$15 + 5 = 20$		$5 + 15 = 20$
etc.		etc.

When trying to make 21, do the children try different pairs of odd numbers and then pairs of even numbers before finding that it cannot be done?

Do they discover that only odd + even = odd, or even + odd = odd?

Section B

A palindrome is a number, word or sentence that reads the same backwards as forwards, for example, '414', 'madam'.

Do the children use a system to make the palindrome 99 by choosing a starting number whose digits add up to 9 – for example, 81, 72, 63, 54, 45, 36, 27, 18 – and then reversing it?

Do any of the children try writing 90 as a starting number? Did reversing it (i.e. 09) cause any difficulties?

Do the children realise that the digits of the starting numbers all add up to 9?

Do the children discover that the palindromes 88, 77, 66, . . . , 11 can be made in a similar way?

Section C

Children will probably use a trial and error approach to begin with.

Do the children understand that they are looking for two-step palindromes? Do they add the numbers correctly?

The children might need a hint that the answer can be found when the sum of the digits is 12 or 13 (or 10). For example,

$75 \rightarrow 12$ $85 \rightarrow 13$ $64 \rightarrow 10$ (The 01 may cause problems.)

Are they systematic in finding all the possibilities?

Do they discover that two-digit numbers whose digits add up to 11 (e.g. 56) are one-step palindromes?

Number 2

Purpose

- To give practice in subtraction bonds by counting on and counting back
- To give practice in subtraction from hundreds, tens and units with decomposition from tens

Materials

Structural apparatus, 100 square, number line

Vocabulary

Take away, difference between, pattern, subtraction, count back, diagram, circle, how many left.

TEACHING POINTS

1 Take away

Talk to the children about 'take away' situations;
'There are 20 children in a class. 7 go to play in the band. How many are left?' $20 - 7 = 13$
'Another 3 go to play in a team. How many are left now?' $13 - 3 = 10$

2 Number sentences

Count how many children are in the class and ask the children to write the number down.

Point to a number of children and ask them to stand up. Ask how many children are left sitting down. Encourage the children to write a number sentence:

$34 - 5 = 29$

Talk about other possible number sentences, such as $\underline{34} - 29 = 5$, $29 + 5 = \underline{34}$, or $5 + 29 = \underline{34}$.

3 Counting back

Use the 100 square or number line to count back the required number of spaces and land on the 'answer'.

Highlight a group of numbers and show the link between addition and subtraction. For example,

11	12	13	14	15	16
21	22	23	24	25	26
31	32	33	34	35	36

and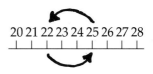

can mean that   22 + 3 = 25
      or   25 − 3 = 22

4 Finding differences

Let the children stand in rows to see the difference in numbers.

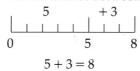

Explain how this can be found by 'counting on'.

The difference between 8 and 5:

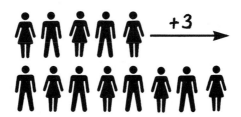

5 + 3 = 8

Talk with the children about other difference situations:
'John has 7 cubes, Jean has 15. What is the difference?'
Show how this can be done by counting on along a number line or by using structural apparatus.

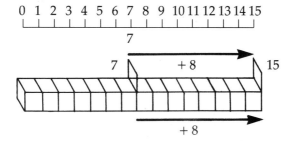

5 Mental work

Let the children subtract single digits from two-digit numbers, for example,

89 − 5,   76 − 3,   39 − 5

Give plenty of practice in this skill and extend the activity by encouraging them to look for patterns, for example,

$$76 - 2, \quad 66 - 2, \quad 56 - 2, \quad \text{etc. or} \quad 74, \quad 64, \quad 54, \quad \text{etc.}$$

Ask the children to subtract mentally in tens ($86 - 10$, $186 - 10$) or in multiples of 10 ($56 - 30$, $74 - 20$). They can also subtract mentally in nines ($25 - 9$, $63 - $) by subtracting 10 and adding 1. This method can be extended to subtracting 19, 29, etc.

6 Recording

Invent some situations to give the children practice in decomposition: There are 353 children in a school and 134 stay to watch a match. How many went home?

Link this with the decomposition method discussed in the Module 4 *Teacher's resource book*, page 116.

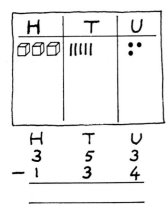

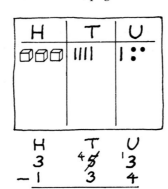

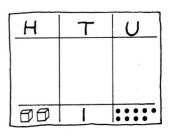

Decomposition can also be shown as a game with children holding up structural apparatus.

Let another child select a card (or throw a die) and physically take that number away from the units. This may require the 'tens' child to hand over one of the tens to the 'units' child so that the child with the card can take the number away.

Draw attention to the final answer and let the children record it.

USING THE CALCULATOR   Revise with the children how to enter three-digit numbers.
Discuss subtraction on the calculator.
Give verbal situations of the type already suggested and let children enter the number sentences on the calculator:
'I have 227 sweets in a jar and give away 9. How many are left?'

A game to play

SHOOT TO 100

This is a game for two players and gives practice in the four rules of number.
The first player enters any number in the calculator, e.g. 274. The second player has to get to 100 (or another chosen number) in three moves. For example,

$$274 - 4 = 270$$
$$270 - 70 = 200$$
$$200 - 100 = 100$$

Some children may come to realise that this can be done in one move:

$$274 - 174 = 100$$

A variation is to use a mixture of $+, -, \div, \times$. This is more difficult.

$$274 - 4 = 270$$
$$270 - 70 = 200$$
$$200 \div 2 = 100$$

or starting at 59:

$$59 + 1 = 60$$
$$60 \times 2 = 120$$
$$120 - 20 = 100$$

LINKS WITH THE ENVIRONMENT

Talk to the children about where subtraction situations occur:
- scoring in games, e.g. darts
- time left (in minutes) on a video tape
- count down on space launch
- going back in board games
- working out how far there is still to travel on a journey (talk about how journeys are still measured in miles in Britain)

NOTES ON INVESTIGATIONS

Section A

Do children see the pattern for the subtraction of nines?

100 91 82 73 64 55 46 37 28 19 10 1

Do they see that the units numbers go through the sequence 0, 1, 2, 3, etc. and the tens numbers through the sequence 0, 9, 8, 7, etc.?
   Do they start at other numbers and find a pattern in the units? For example,

88 79 70 61 52 43 34 25 16 7

Section B

Do the children realise that there are many possible answers, with the top number in the units column one greater than the number in the bottom column?

9 8 7 6 5 4 3 2 1
8 7 6 5 4 3 2 1 0
(The number in the tens column of the bottom line is 8 each time.)

$$\begin{array}{r} 3\,{}^{8}\!\not{9}\,{}^{1}0 \\ 1\ 7\ 9 \\ \hline 2\ 1\ 1 \end{array}$$

   Do they go on to discover that there is another answer if decomposition is used?

Section C

Do the children approach the problem in a logical way? For example, do they complete the corners first?

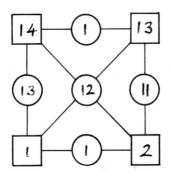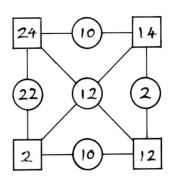

shape 1

Purpose

- To use a mirror to show line symmetry
- To use symmetry to complete shapes
- To recognise types of movement
- To recognise planes of symmetry

Materials

Double-sided mirrors, squared paper, tracing paper

Vocabulary

Dotted line, symmetry, mirror, whole shape, line of symmetry, design, square, rectangle, reflect, reflection, rotate

TEACHING POINTS

1 What is symmetry?

Revise the idea that a symmetrical shape has a line or axis of symmetry, and can be divided into two halves which are reflections of each other.

2 Symmetry in nature

Ask for suggestions of shapes in nature that appear to be symmetrical, such as a butterfly, bird, insect, tortoise, leaf and flowers. Can the children think of reasons why creatures are mostly symmetrical? Look for parts which are symmetrical like wings or legs, and for parts which are not symmetrical. Markings on creatures are often almost symmetrical, but not quite.

Talk about how birds and animals need symmetry to fly and move. What would happen if an animal had legs longer on one side than on the other?

Do creatures always have symmetry of colour? Discuss with the children whether they have symmetry. Do clothes have symmetry of shape and colour?

3 Using a mirror to show symmetry (vertical line)

Draw some pictures and mark on each the line of symmetry.

Show the children how to place the mirror on the line. What do they see? What do they see if they look in the other side of the mirror?

4 Horizontal lines of symmetry

Draw pictures which have a horizontal line of symmetry. Ask the children to look in both sides of the mirror.

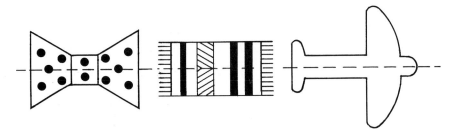

5 Lack of symmetry

When the children are confident in the use of the mirror to find symmetry, show them some pictures which do not have symmetry. Let them draw what they see when they look in each side of the mirror.

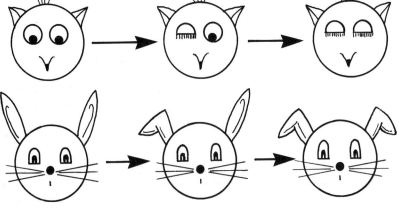

Let the children draw faces which don't have symmetry.

6 Funny faces

This activity can be fun. Give the children a picture of half a face, with the line of symmetry shown. Ask them to use their mirrors to draw the complete face. Some children might find tracing paper useful for completing the shapes.

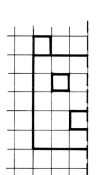

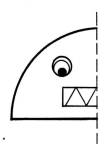

Let the children draw half a face or shape with a line of symmetry for, a friend to complete, using a mirror. Squared paper might be helpful for accuracy in drawing.

7 Making patterns

Let the children make patterns using the idea of symmetry.

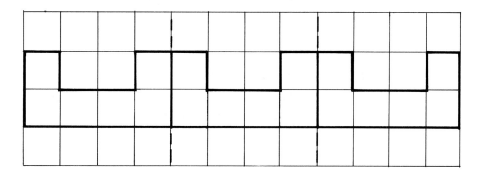

8 Types of movement

Talk about different types of movement. Let the children draw pictures or patterns using a template. For example:

Straight movement (translation)

Turning movement (rotation)

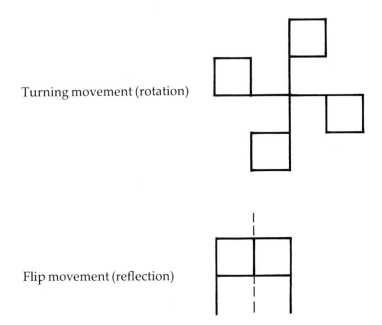

Flip movement (reflection)

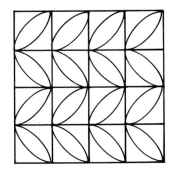

Art and craft lessons are a good time to discuss the different types of movement, when prints with objects can be used to make patterns.

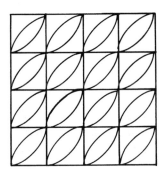 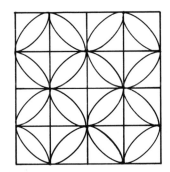

9 Planes of symmetry

With three-dimensional shapes we talk about planes rather than lines of symmetry.

Talk about symmetry in three-dimensional shapes, such as boxes and cylinders. Ask the children to tell you where the planes of symmetry are.

Make a cube of plasticine. Ask the children to find ways of cutting it to make two equal pieces. To do this, they need to decide which are the planes of symmetry. For example,

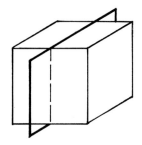 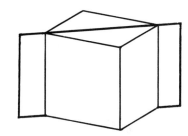 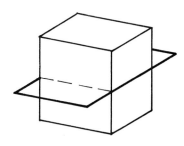

LINKS WITH THE ENVIRONMENT

- Consider symmetry in the environment. Look at tree shapes, leaves, flowers, plants. Do they have symmetry?
- Look at animals. Do they have symmetry of shape? Do they have symmetry of colour?
- Do buildings have symmetry? Look at houses near school. Look at doors, windows and other parts of buildings.
- Consider symmetry in pattern work. Let the children build up symmetrical patterns using templates. Ask them to show the lines of symmetry.
- Reflections on water
- Road signs in the Highway Code
- Look at boxes, containers, tins and bottles for planes of symmetry. A collection can be made and displayed in the classroom.

NOTES ON INVESTIGATIONS

Section A

Do the children understand that they have to complete a rectangle to give the pattern symmetry? Do they use the same colour for these two extra squares? Do they consider symmetry of both shape and colour when adding the extra squares?

Section B

Does the first flag have symmetry (vertical line)? Does the second flag have symmetry (horizontal line)? Does the third flag have any symmetry?

Do any of the children think of drawing half a flag first and then completing it using a mirror or tracing paper?

Section C

Do the children carefully position the mirror to produce the required number of squares? Can they think of a way to record this? One method might be:

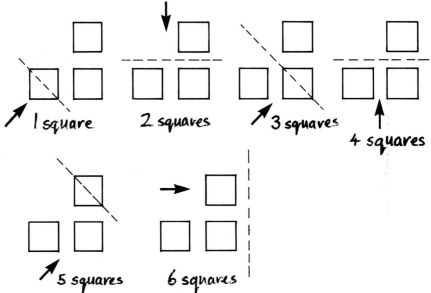

The arrow shows the direction of sight.

Number 3

Purpose

- To introduce the tables of 6 and 9
- To discover patterns of multiplication
- To multiply two digits by one digit
- To link multiplication and addition

Materials

Structural apparatus, squared paper, 100 square

Vocabulary

Pattern, digit, multiply, tables, odd, even, 100 square, answers

TEACHING POINTS   **1 Sets of six**

Talk about where sets of six are found:
- Insects have six legs
- A cube has six faces
- A hexagon has six edges
- Six eggs in a box
- Six stumps needed on a cricket pitch

2 Building up sixes – a game to play

A calculator may be used.

Ask one child to think of an object or shape connected with six, for example, a hexagon. Ask another to give a number less than 10, say 5. Now the children work out how many sides on 5 hexagons.

This is a good opportunity to link + and ×.

$$6 + 6 + 6 + 6 + 6 = 30$$
$$5 \times 6 = 30$$

Repeat this activity, perhaps introducing humorous objects, such as 'how many eyes on the hexapods?'

a 'hexapod'

3 Looking for nines

Ask the children to think about where we find or see nines:

- A rounders team has nine players
- 999 emergency phone number
- House numbers
- 'A cat has nine lives'
- A game of noughts and crosses uses nine spaces
- On a clock face (School starts at 9 o'clock)
- 'How many children in this class are nine years old?'
- September is the 9th month of the year
- 'A stitch in time saves nine'

4 Using a 100 line or square

Let the children count on in nines on a number line, square or board.

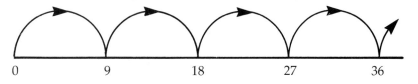

Ask questions related to this:
'What are three nines? What are four nines?' etc.

Link addition and multiplication: $9 + 9 + 9 = 3 \times 9 = 27$

5 Finger multiplication

Use fingers to show the nine times table. For example, to find 4×9, hold down the fourth finger and read off 36.

6 Pattern

Talk about the pattern of nines when adding on in nines. The units digits form a pattern: 9 8 7 6 5 4 3 2 1 0
Also the tens digits: 1 2 3 4 5 6 7 8 9

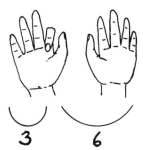

3   6

7 Mental work

Revise with children the quick way of adding on nine (or finding multiples of nine). Adding nine is the same as adding ten and subtracting one.

$$27 + 9$$
$$27 + 10 - 1$$
$$37 - 1 = 36$$

Point out that when we add nine the new last digit is one less than before (0 should be discussed as an exception).

8 Multiplication of two digits by one digit

Revise the method of recording:

```
 H   T   U
     2   5
X_____6
_____
```

Use your own form of words to deal with the 'carrying' process, so that children understand it. This will also apply to the positioning of the 'carried' number.
Use structural apparatus to let children become familiar with the imagery.

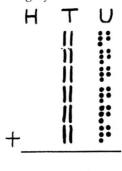

USING THE CALCULATOR Use the constant function on the calculator to build up the tables of 6 and 9. Then let the children start at any number. For example, start on 4 and add on in 6 or 9. Talk about the patterns.

4	10	16	22	28	34	40	46	52	58	64
4	13	22	31	40	49	58	67	76	85	94

Ask the children to look at the last digit each time and talk about the patterns.

A game to play

USE THE NUMBERS

Two players take it in turns to turn over four cards from a shuffled pack marked 0 to 9. Each player tries to get as close to 100 as possible using the same four numbers once only and the signs $\times$ and $+$. For example:

The numbers 5, 7, 2, 3 are turned over.

The first player enters $3 \times 27 + 5 = 86$.

The second player enters $75 + 23 = 98$.

The second player scores 1 point.

The cards are shuffled again and four new cards turned over for the next round.

The winner is the first player to score ten points.

LINKS WITH THE ENVIRONMENT

- Look in the shops for things sold in sixes and nines, for example, bars of chocolate, biscuits in boxes.
- Look at bus numbers and see if the route number is in the table of six or nine.
- Look at class sizes in your school. Are any of the numbers multiples of six or nine?

NOTES ON INVESTIGATIONS

Section A

Do the children see the patterns emerging on the 100 square? Do they realise that the patterns allow them to predict the next numbers?

1	2	3	4	5	6	7	8	9	10
11	12	13	14	15	16	17	18	19	20
21	22	23	24	25	26	27	28	29	30
31	32	33	34	35	36	37	38	39	40
41	42	43	44	45	46	47	48	49	50
51	52	53	54	55	56	57	58	59	60
61	62	63	64	65	66	67	68	69	70
71	72	73	74	75	76	77	78	79	80
81	82	83	84	85	86	87	88	89	90
91	92	93	94	95	96	97	98	99	100

1	2	3	4	5	6	7	8	9	10
11	12	13	14	15	16	17	18	19	20
21	22	23	24	25	26	27	28	29	30
31	32	33	34	35	36	37	38	39	40
41	42	43	44	45	46	47	48	49	50
51	52	53	54	55	56	57	58	59	60
61	62	63	64	65	66	67	68	69	70
71	72	73	74	75	76	77	78	79	80
81	82	83	84	85	86	87	88	89	90
91	92	93	94	95	96	97	98	99	100

Do they investigate what happens if they start at different numbers? For example, 4? Do they recognise similar patterns?

1	2	3	4	5	6	7	8	9	10
11	12	13	14	15	16	17	18	19	20
21	22	23	24	25	26	27	28	29	30
31	32	33	34	35	36	37	38	39	40
41	42	43	44	45	46	47	48	49	50
51	52	53	54	55	56	57	58	59	60
61	62	63	64	65	66	67	68	69	70
71	72	73	74	75	76	77	78	79	80
81	82	83	84	85	86	87	88	89	90
91	92	93	94	95	96	97	98	99	100

Section B

A calculator may be used. Do the children adopt a logical approach? Do they, for example, restrict themselves to two numbers to begin with? Do they find the relationships

odd $\times$ odd = odd
even $\times$ even = even
even $\times$ odd = even
odd $\times$ even = even

$\times$	odd	even
odd	odd	even
even	even	even

Do they go on to try multiplying three numbers:

$$\text{odd} \times \text{odd} \times \text{odd} = \text{odd}$$

Do they realise that multiplying odd numbers will always produce odd numbers and multiplying even numbers always produces even numbers?

Section C

Do the children see that the initial pattern is going up in tens and that the last digit is always 9?

When they multiply by 2, do they see that the pattern goes up in twenties and that the last digit is always 8?   18   38   58   78   98.

When they multiply by 4, do they see that the pattern goes up in forties and that the last digit is always 6?   36   76   116   156   196.

Do they find the pattern when they multiply by 5?

Do they experiment with other patterns? For example,   7   17   27   37   47   57   Do they see that similar patterns emerge?

Area 1

Purpose

- To find the area of irregular shapes by counting squares
- To introduce the half square method for finding the area of shapes

Materials

Squared paper, tracing paper

Vocabulary

Area, whole squares, half squares, grids, less, same size, count, estimate, three pieces, rearrange, twice as long

TEACHING POINTS

1 What is area?

Revise the idea that area is the amount of surface covered by a shape. Remind the children that we can measure area by counting squares. Do they remember why we use squares and not circles?

2 Revision of counting whole squares

Ask the children to draw a shape of area 15 squares, say, on squared paper, and record its area. (Use areas less than 25 squares.)

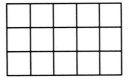

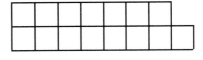

Area = 15 squares

Area = 15 squares

Talk about the different shapes they draw with the same area. Stress the idea that one area can take many shapes.

3 Revision of counting in half squares

Ask the children to draw shapes or pictures as in the last activity, but this time they must include half squares.

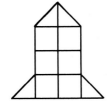

Area = 8 squares

4 Introducing the half square method

Talk about how the area of irregular shapes can be found. For example,

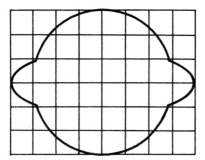

Show the children how to count the squares:

- count all the whole squares
- count half (or greater) squares as whole squares
- don't count anything less than half a square

Explain how this gives an approximate, though usually quite accurate, answer.

5 Using a grid sheet

Show the children how to use a square grid on a transparent sheet (or one marked on tracing paper) to measure the area of irregular shapes.

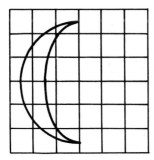  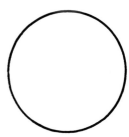

LINKS WITH THE ENVIRONMENT

- Look for areas of tiles or carpet squares in school or shops.
- Area can be linked to pattern and display work.
- Consider area in the animal world, for example, increased foot area of animals such as camels and polar bears who walk on sand or ice. Talk about the increased surface area of animals' ears in hot climates – for example, the desert fox – and the reduced area of ears of animals in cold climates – for example, the arctic fox (the area affects heat loss from the body).

NOTES ON INVESTIGATIONS

Section A

It is useful to have a set of 5 cm × 3 cm grids marked out on larger sheets of squared paper and duplicated ready for the children's use.

Do the children draw capital letters?

Do they first draw one letter, count its area and continue to draw others until they find one with the same area? Or do they estimate which letters might have the same area and try those first?

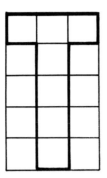

Do any children draw curved letters and use the half square counting method?

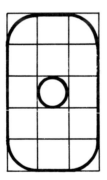

Section B

The 5 cm × 3 cm grids will be useful here.

Do the children realise that letters such as b, d, p, q are similar and will have the same area?

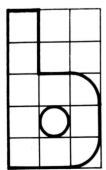 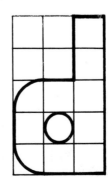 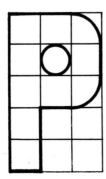 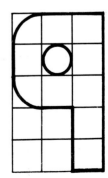

Section C

Do the children have difficulty in doubling the size of the letters?

Are they surprised that the area is four times greater rather than just doubled?

The investigation can be extended by asking the children to double the dimensions of any shape drawn. The area will again be four times greater.

Number 4

Purpose

- To introduce division by 6 and 9
- To show the link between multiplication and division
- To introduce division of tens and units by one digit

Materials

Structural apparatus, squared paper

Vocabulary

Division, divide exactly, remainder, row, answer, number square, table charts

TEACHING POINTS

1 Division by 6

Talk about grouping in sixes. Ask the children to draw objects (or use counters) to show multiples of 6, for example, 12.

'How many sixes are there?'
Show the grouping.

Talk about ways of recording this.

$$12 \div 6 = \qquad 6\overline{)12} \qquad \frac{12}{6}$$

Draw the table of six. Talk about the patterns – the numbers down increase by 6, the numbers across are alternate odd/even.

1	2	3	4	5	6
7	8	9	10	11	12
13	14	15	16	17	18
19	20	21	22	23	24
25	26	27	28	29	30
31	32	33	34	35	36
37	38	39	40	41	42
43	44	45	46	47	48
49	50	51	52	53	54
55	56	57	58	59	60

Ask the children to count in sixes from the table, for example,

6, 12, 18, 24, 30, 36, 42, 48, 54, 60

Talk about the sixes number pattern

- The last digits of the numbers repeat 6, 2, 8, 4, 0,   6, 2, 8, 4, 0.
- The sums of the digits are all multiples of 3.

Use the table and ask, 'How many sixes in 24?' – show that there are four groups of 6. Talk about ways of recording this.

$$24 \div 6 = 4 \qquad 6\overline{)24}^{\,4} \qquad \frac{24}{6} = 4$$

Repeat this for other numbers.

2 Division by 9

Repeat the previous activities to show division by 9.

The pattern of 9 can be written as:

$9 \rightarrow 9$
$18 \rightarrow 9$
$27 \rightarrow 9$
$36 \rightarrow 9$
$45 \rightarrow 9$
$54 \rightarrow 9$
$63 \rightarrow 9$
$72 \rightarrow 9$
$81 \rightarrow 9$
$90 \rightarrow 9$

The sums of the pairs of digits add up to 9.

Use the information from the pattern and ask, 'How many 9s in 63?'

Let the children use their fingers to count down the last digit of each number in the pattern of 9 until they reach 6 i.e. 9, 8, 7, 6. 6 is the last digit of 36. They have used four fingers so there are four 9s in 36. Do this with other numbers in the table of 9.

3 Link multiplication and division

Talk about the link between multiplication and division, i.e. $3 \times 6 = 18$ and $18 \div 6 = 3$. This can be shown using squared paper.

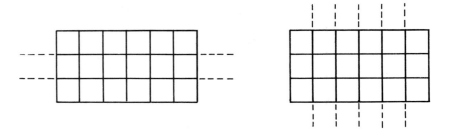

Show that the relationship between the numbers 3, 6 and 18 can be written in four ways.

$$3 \times 6 = 18 \qquad 6 \times 3 = 18 \qquad 18 \div 3 = 6 \qquad 18 \div 6 = 3$$

Ask the children to write four number bonds for other sets of numbers, for example, 2, 6, 12 or 3, 9, 27.

A game to play

BALLOON BONDS

Make several balloon cards like this, and cup up the balloons into four pieces.

Shuffle all the different pieces face down on the table.

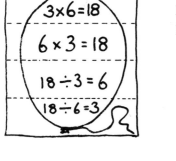

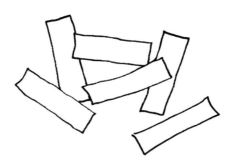

Players take turns to pick up one piece and make up balloons. If a piece is not wanted it can be returned, face down, to its place on the table. The winner is the one with the most completed balloons.

4 Division of tens and units by one digit

Use structural apparatus to show the meaning of division (no changing). For example,

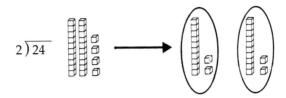

Talk about the method of recording 2) 24. Use your usual form of words to explain sharing into two equal groups.

Use structural apparatus to explain division when 'changing' is involved. For example,

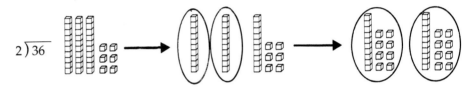

Talk about the recording of this.

$$2 \overline{\smash{)}\, 3^1 6}$$
$$\phantom{2 \overline{)}}\ 1\ 8$$

Use structural apparatus to give the children the imagery.

5 Mental work

Give the children practice in using multiplication and division bonds. For example, $18 \div 2 = \square$, $18 \div 9 = \square$, $2 \times 9 = \square$, and $9 \times 2 = \square$.

Ask the children division problems. For example,
'If there are twelve sweets how many would three children get each?'
'If there are thirteen sweets how many would be left over?'

USING THE CALCULATOR

1 Practise division by 6 and 9

Switch on your calculator.

Enter   4   2

Press the ÷

Press   6

Press the =

Read off your answer.

Set these problems in a real situation wherever possible.

2 Remainders

Let the children practise division by 2, 3 and 4. For example, $24 \div 2$
$27 \div 2$

The question of remainders will arise and many teachers will feel
that this is not the time to discuss decimal notation. It is probably
sufficient to explain that if the answer has numbers after the point
(other than 0 on some calculators) the number does not divide exactly.

A game to play

FIND A DIVISION

This is a game for two or more players who will need counters, a
calculator and a grid like this:

2	3	4	5	6
7	8	9	10	12
14	15	16	18	20
24	25	27	28	30

The first player chooses any number on the grid. The second player
then tries to make up exact divisions for the number using the
calculator. One point is scored for each correct division made. For
example,

15 gives $15 \div 3 = 5$ (1 point)

6 gives $6 \div 3 = 2$
$6 \div 2 = 3$
$6 \div 1 = 6$
$6 \div 6 = 1$ (4 points)

The 'used' number is then covered with a counter or crossed off the
grid. The players then change over.

The winner is the player with the most points when all the numbers
on the grid have been used.

The numbers on the grid may be chosen according to the ability of
the children playing.

**LINKS WITH THE
ENVIRONMENT**

• Talk about sharing or grouping situations in everyday life. For
example, sharing sweets or money.

- At school children may be put in PE teams of 6 or play games like rounders with 9 children in each team.
- At cub-scouts or brownie-guides, children are grouped in sixes.

**NOTES ON
INVESTIGATIONS**

Section A

Do the children realise that the missing numbers for $2\overline{)7\square}$ must be all even (i.e. 0, 2, 4, 6, 8) and that odd numbers would give remainders?

Are the children systematic in finding different possible numbers for $2\overline{)\square 4}$? Do they try even numbers first (i.e. 24, 44, 64, 84) and then find 14, 34, 54, 74 and 94? Or do they realise that because the last digit is even any number from 1 to 9 is a possible answer?

Section B

Are the children systematic in finding different answers?

Do they use the link between multiplication and division? For example, $2 \times 3 = 6$, $3 \times 2 = 6$, $6 \div 3 = 2$, $6 \div 2 = 3$.

Do they use the commutative law? For example, $2 \times 6 = 12$ and $6 \times 2 = 12$.

Section C

Do the children use a systematic approach? For example, do they write out the patterns of 3, 6 and 9 and compare them?

Do any children realise that 3 is a factor of both 6 and 9 and will therefore divide exactly into any multiple of the others? Do they just use the larger number (i.e. 9) to try to find a pattern of numbers which will also divide by 6 and 3 (i.e. 18, 36, 54, 72, 90, . . .)?

In finding numbers which will divide exactly by 2, 3 and 5, do the children write the patterns of 2, 3 and 5 and compare them? Do they realise that the numbers must be even because of division by 2? Having found the first number, 30, do any of the children realise that the other numbers must be in a pattern – 30, 60, 90 etc?

The investigation can be extended by using other combinations of numbers, for example, 3, 4, 5.

Data 1

Purpose

- To use block graphs or bar charts and the 1:2 scale
- To introduce the 1:10 scale
- To give practice in interpreting graphs
- To use charts to classify data

Materials

1 cm and 2 cm squared paper

Vocabulary

Graph, half, twice, order, most, fewest, title, labels, questions, block graph, bar chart, chart, numbers, table

TEACHING POINTS

1 Graphs

Remind the children that graphs are a way of showing data or information in an easy-to-read form. Ask them to design a data collection sheet, perhaps using tallying, to show how they come to school. Ask them then to draw a graph in the form of a block graph or bar chart. Remind them about writing the labels, numbers, and the title for the graph.

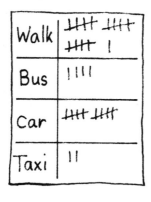
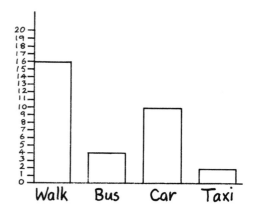

Give the children practice in obtaining information from graphs. For example, make a class graph of favourite animals and ask the children to suggest suitable questions based on the graph for other children to answer. Ask them what would happen to the graph if it had been made by another class. Would it have exactly the same number and animals?

2 Revise the 1:2 scale

Ask the children what would happen if the 1:1 graph had been for two classes of children and so the numbers had doubled. The graph would go off the page! Talk about how the 1:2 scale would be better and draw the graph again, using this scale.

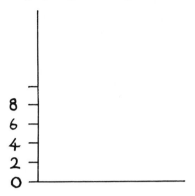

3 Larger numbers

Talk to the children about when the numbers are larger still. For example:

- Number of children in school
- Traffic survey on a busy road
- Heights of children in cm

Ask how such numbers can be shown on squared paper. Of course, a very large sheet of squared paper could be used, but would this be practical? Can anyone suggest a better way?

Discuss using a 1:10 scale and normal sized squared paper.

4 The 1:10 scale

Draw a graph using the 1:10 scale.

Talk about where numbers like 15 and 35 are. Ask the children to explain where 18 is and why.

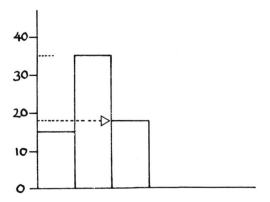

5 Comparing scales

Talk about graphs with different scales. Give the chidren practice in reading them and discuss how it is easier to read numbers like 18 on a 1:1 scale.

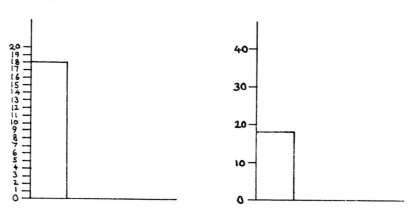

6 Diagrams showing data

Talk with the children about sorting data and how this can be shown. Draw a tree or branching diagram and talk about sorting shapes.

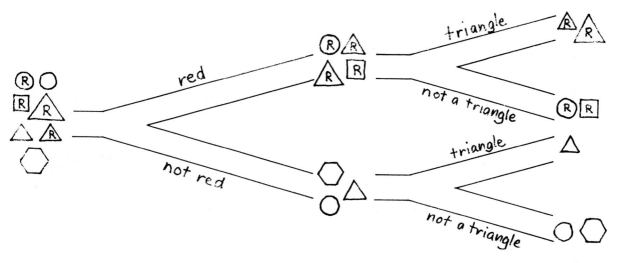

Turn this into a game by asking the children to design 'routes' of their own. Read the instructions to a friend and see if they end up in the right place.

Lewis Carroll (author of *Alice in Wonderland*) devised the Carroll diagram to sort data. Talk about showing data on one of these diagrams. Ask the children to describe what is in each section. Ask them to design a Carroll diagram of their own.

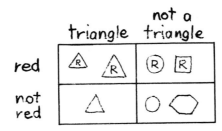

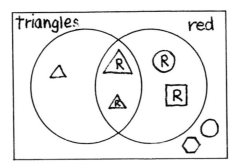

Data can also be shown on a Venn diagram. Ask the children to say where particular shapes would go and why. Ask them to design their own Venn diagrams.

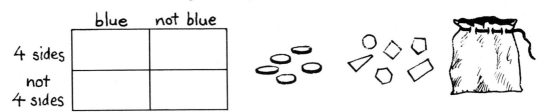

A game to play

PLACE IT

You need a board with a Carroll diagram marked, some counters, and some shapes in a bag.

Children play in teams of 2 to 4. In turn, the children take a shape from the bag and place it in the correct section of the Carroll diagram. They collect one counter for their team if they place the shape correctly.

The first team to collect 6 counters are the winners.

7 Mental work

Talk about the outcomes of events. Discuss, for example, whether events are certain, uncertain or impossible:

- It will be sunny tomorrow.
- It will be Saturday tomorrow.
- It will get dark tonight.
- I will be 100 years old at dinner time.

Play a game

CERTAIN OR NOT!

Write ⌐certain⌐, ⌐uncertain⌐ and ⌐impossible⌐ on three equal sized pieces of card. Place the cards face down and shuffle them.

One child picks up one card, and chooses a friend to make up an outcome or event to match with the word on the card. If it is correct, then that child can choose a card, and a friend to make up an event.

The rest of the children can act as judges.

LINKS WITH THE ENVIRONMENT

Use opportunities in school to produce meaningful graphs or charts.

- Fund raising. Show amounts collected on a graph or chart.
- Sports day scores. Team scores may be displayed on a data collection sheet. For example, cricket, rounders or unihoc scores.
- A traffic census can be shown as a graph.
- Look for graphs and charts in newspapers and magazines.
- Weather. Keep an on-going graph of rainy days, sunny days, dull days, etc.
- Books. The children can make graphs or diagrams about the different sorts of books in the classroom.

NOTES ON INVESTIGATIONS

Section A

Do the children choose books that will fit in all sections of the Carroll diagram? Do they write appropriate questions that fit the information?

Section B

Do the children consider suitable titles for the graph, such as ones where numbers of this size might be expected? Do they finish the graph and label it correctly?

Are their questions sensible? Are any of the questions open-ended?

Section C

Do the children draw two different graphs or charts? Do they realise that there are various features that they might use? For example, book colour, size or type of animal.

Money 1

Purpose

- To practise addition and subtraction of pounds and pence with 'carrying'
- To give practice in working out bills and change
- To make up amounts of money using coins

Materials

Coins

Vocabulary

Total cost, bill, money left, coins, change, large, medium, small, magic square, buy, amount, to price, exactly, add

TEACHING POINTS

1 Coin values

Remind the children of the coin values. Give them practice in making up amounts of money.
Make some cards:

Set A

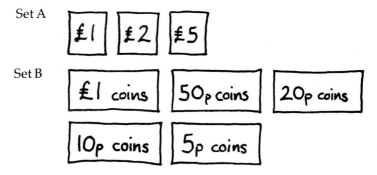

Set B

Put set A in one box and set B in another. Ask a child to choose one card from each box and to give you the amount in the coins stated, for example, £2 in 10p coins.
This may be extended by including £3 and £4 in set A.
Let the children make simple charts by drawing round coins or make up plastic bank bags of money.

2 Splitting £ and p

Remind the children of the importance of the point to separate the £ and the pence. Without it, people will not know what the amount is worth. For example, 365 could be £3.65 or £36.5 or £365.

Write amounts of money for children to change from pence to £ and vice versa.

3 Adding bills

Revise the word 'bill', and how to total bills.

Give the children practice either with a simple wall shop or cards with pictures and prices on.

Remind the children how to write bills. For example,

$$
\begin{array}{r}
£ \\
2 \cdot 25 \\
+ 1 \cdot 49 \\
\hline
\end{array}
$$

4 What's left?

Give the children further practice, using the wall shop or shopping cards as for Activity 3 above. Give a child a purse holding an amount of plastic money – enough to exceed the bill. Ask them to work out their bill and then hand over the money. How much is left in the purse?

5 Subtraction

Discuss subtraction of money. Remind the children how to use decomposition.

$$
\begin{array}{r}
£ \\
4 \cdot {}^{5}6{}^{1}0 \\
- 1 \cdot 2\ 7 \\
\hline
\end{array}
$$

Show the children how they can check their answers with the calculator.

6 Mental work

Give the children mental work involving money. For example,

- Addition – adding small amounts of money.

- Coin values – let the children say which coins they might use to make given amounts of money.
- Simple change – give the children practice in working out change mentally. A good way to do this is 'shopkeeper's' addition:

I have 10p. I pay 6p. My change is 4p.
6p + 1p + 1p + 1p + 1p = 10p
4p

7 Games to play

BANK GAME

Two children can play this game. One is the cashier. The other chooses a card with an amount of money on it, and hands it to the cashier who pays the amount in coins. The cashier scores one point for every correct amount given.

The children change places after several turns.

CAFÉ GAME

Paper plates have 'meals' coloured on them, with prices, for customers to buy with a given amount of money. The waiter adds up the bill and the customer pays. The waiter may need to give change.

A calculator can be used as a check.

BAG RACE

This can be a team game.

Ask two players, one from each team, to fill a bag with a given amount of money, for example, £3 in 20p coins. The first to hand in the bag with the correct number of coins scores the point.

USING THE CALCULATOR

Show the children how to enter pounds and pence, using the decimal point, for example, £3.52 as 3.52.

Point out that if the calculator shows £1.8 this means £1.80 (one pound and eighty pence).

Remind the children how to use the calculator for working out bills and change.

Use the constant function to count how many 20p coins in, for example, £2 (200p). As well as counting on, the constant function may be used to count down in 20p coins from £2.

LINKS WITH THE ENVIRONMENT

- Collect money bags from banks and discuss how many of each coin they should hold. Collect 'savings sticks' designed to hold particular coins and discuss these.
- Talk about pocket money with the children – how they spend it and save it.
- Talk about the cost of going out for the day. What are the costs and what are the bills? Talk about buying petrol, having a snack, buying tickets to get in places, etc. Is there such a thing as a 'cheap day out' for families?

NOTES ON INVESTIGATIONS

Section A

Do the children use a system? Do they, for example, start by collecting all the possible coins? Do they then use the first two, or any two, and exhaust all the possibilities before going on?

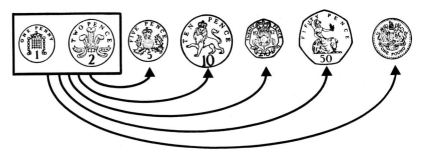

Do they use the correct notation when recording their amounts? An extension is to use four coins.

Section B

Do the children use a system? Two possible methods are:

  51p, 52p and make up to 175p
  51p, 53p and make up to 175p
   and so on

or

  split into three 50ps and divide the remaining 25p amongst the three amounts.

Section C

Do the children realise that the £1 is a good starting coin? Possible answers are:

120p:	£1	10p	5p	5p
121p:	£1	10p	10p	1p
122p:	£1	10p	10p	2p
123p:	£1	20p	2p	1p
124p:	£1	20p	2p	2p
125p:	£1	10p	10p	5p
126p:	£1	20p	5p	1p
127p:	£1	20p	5p	2p
128p:	not possible			
129p:	not possible			
130p:	£1	20p	5p	5p

All values are possible with five coins.

Number 5

Purpose

- To revise the equivalence of fractions ($1 = \frac{4}{4} = \frac{2}{2}$, $\frac{1}{2} = \frac{2}{4}$)
- To introduce the addition of half and quarter

Materials

Squared paper

Vocabulary

Half, halves, whole, number sentence, rectangles, symmetry, quarter

TEACHING POINTS   **1 Revise $\frac{1}{2}$, $\frac{1}{4}$, $\frac{3}{4}$**

Remind the children that $\frac{1}{2}$ means one part out of two equal parts, $\frac{1}{4}$ means one part out of four equal parts, $\frac{3}{4}$ means 3 parts out of 4 equal parts.

Talk with them about halves, quarters and three-quarters of various shapes. Use shapes like these and ask the children to colour $\frac{1}{2}$ red or $\frac{1}{4}$ blue. Ask, 'What fraction is left?' or 'What fraction is coloured?'

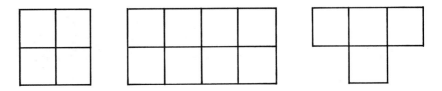

Revise the recording of $\frac{1}{2}, \frac{1}{4}, \frac{3}{4}$. Talk about what they mean.
Check that the children do not confuse $\frac{3}{4}$ with $3\frac{1}{4}$.

Ask the children to draw a shape of their own on squared paper and colour $\frac{1}{2}, \frac{1}{4}$ or $\frac{3}{4}$.
Ask the children to find halves, quarters and three-quarters of numbers of objects, for example,

2 Mental work

Ask the children to work out:

$\frac{1}{2}$ of 2, 4, 6, 8, 10, 12, 14, 16, 18, 20.
$\frac{1}{4}$ of 4, 8, 12, 16, 20.
$\frac{3}{4}$ of 4, 8, 12, 16, 20 (for those able to cope with this).

3 Equivalence of fractions

Draw a fraction wall or ask the children to make one using squared paper or strips.

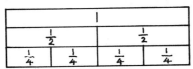

Talk about the equivalences.
'How many halves in 1?'
'How many quarters in 1?'
'How many quarters in one-half?'
Talk about the recording.

$$1 = \tfrac{2}{2}, \quad 1 = \tfrac{4}{4}, \quad \tfrac{1}{2} = \tfrac{2}{4}$$

Give the children three squares. Ask them to mark '1' or '1 whole' on the first. Fold the second into halves and mark each half. Fold the third square into quarters and mark each quarter. Talk about the recording in symbols and words.

Mark equivalent fractions on the reverse of the square and talk about them. Make mobiles of equivalent fractions to hang up in the classroom.

4 Addition of halves

Talk with the children about adding halves. Show this with shapes.

Show the recording:

$\frac{1}{2} + \frac{1}{2} = 1$

Use the fraction wall to show $\frac{1}{2} + \frac{1}{2} = 1$.

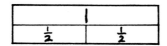

5 Addition of quarters

Talk with the children about adding quarters. Show this with the square or fraction wall.

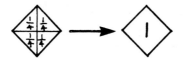
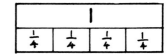

Talk about the recording

$\frac{1}{4} + \frac{1}{4} + \frac{1}{4} + \frac{1}{4} = 1$

Talk about $\frac{1}{4} + \frac{1}{4} = \frac{2}{4}$ and $\frac{1}{4} + \frac{1}{4} + \frac{1}{4} = \frac{3}{4}$.

6 Addition of a half and a quarter

Show the children how to add $\frac{1}{2} + \frac{1}{4}$ using diagrams or the fraction wall.

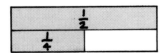

Explain that we only add fractions with the same denominator, and some fractions need to be changed to an equivalent.

$$\frac{1}{2} + \frac{1}{4} =$$
$$\frac{2}{4} + \frac{1}{4} = \frac{3}{4}$$

Then talk about the addition $\frac{1}{4} + \frac{1}{2}$ in the same way.

Ask the children to draw $\frac{1}{2} + \frac{1}{4}$ of various shapes.

Ask 'What fraction is left?'

USING THE CALCULATOR

Show the children how we can find $\frac{1}{2}$, $\frac{1}{4}$ and $\frac{3}{4}$ of numbers using the calculator. For example, to find $\frac{1}{2}$ of 8 we divide 8 by 2: $\boxed{8}$ $\boxed{\div}$ $\boxed{2}$ $\boxed{=}$

To find $\frac{1}{4}$ of 12 we divide 12 by 4: $\boxed{12}$ $\boxed{\div}$ $\boxed{4}$ $\boxed{=}$

To find $\frac{3}{4}$ of 12 we find $\frac{1}{4}$ of 12 and then add the answer three times, because $\frac{1}{4} + \frac{1}{4} + \frac{1}{4} = \frac{3}{4}$.

NB. The numbers must be carefully chosen in order to avoid decimals when dividing.

LINKS WITH THE ENVIRONMENT

Talk with the children about where we see $\frac{1}{2}$, $\frac{1}{4}$ and $\frac{3}{4}$ of shapes or numbers in everyday life.

- We might share cake, chocolate, sweets, fruit or rock into these fractions.
- Halves and quarters are used in telling the time. For example, half past, quarter past, quarter to, $\frac{1}{2}$ an hour, $\frac{1}{4}$ of an hour, $\frac{3}{4}$ of an hour.

- Patterns, flags or shields may be divided into halves and quarters.

NOTES ON INVESTIGATIONS

Section A

A supply of ready-made circles is useful for folding into accurate fractions.

Check that the children know what a pizza is, and are aware that it is usually circular.

If they colour halves like this:

do they see that the shape has been rotated?

Do the children realise that $\frac{1}{2}$ can also be coloured like this?

Do the children understand that $\frac{3}{4}$ can be shown in only two ways but can obviously be coloured in many ways?

Section B

Do the children find all possible combinations of number sentence?

Do any of them record $\frac{1}{2} + \frac{1}{2} = \frac{2}{2}$ or $\frac{2}{4} + \frac{2}{4} = \frac{4}{4}$, which are both correct?

Do their pictures match up with their number sentences?

Section C

Do the children realise that $\frac{1}{2}$ of 12 = 6 and $\frac{1}{4}$ of 12 = 3?

Do their rectangles have lines of symmetry?

Do they realise that half squares need to be considered with both vertical and horizontal lines of symmetry?

Do they produce a variety of answers?

Length 1

Purpose

- To measure in centimetres (cm) and metres (m)
- To give practice in estimating

Materials

Tape measures, trundle wheel, metre stick

Vocabulary

Measure, measurements, estimate, length, longer, high, higher, reach, height, metre, trundle wheel, straight, size, nearest metre, centimetre, shortest, shorter, tape measure, stretch, sizes, straight

TEACHING POINTS

1 Measuring ourselves

Talk to children about why it is important to be measured for clothes. What happens if the measurements are wrong? What would it look like if a child was given a coat made for an adult?

Do the children know someone who knits or sews? How do they measure to see if the garment fits? Do they use a tape measure or fit it against the person?

How do we know the size of bought clothes? Let the children look for labels in their clothes. Do the labels give ages or measurements?

2 Centimetre tape measures

Show the children tape measures marked in centimetres and talk about how to use them. How many cm long are they?

Give practice in using tape measures.

- Let children measure their cubits or head circumference with a tape measure.
- Show them how to measure their stride by marking it on the floor and then using the tape measure. These results may be used for graph work.

Ask the children to describe what they have done.

3 Estimating in cm

Estimating is an important skill. When children have had considerable practice in measuring in cm, they should be encouraged to estimate the length of objects before checking their estimate with a tape measure.

Let them look at clothes and estimate which members of the class they might fit. Can they give the approximate measurement for a jumper to fit a friend?

4 Estimating and measuring in metres

Show the children a metre stick and talk to them about estimating distances.

Ask them to estimate the length of the classroom in metres. This can then be measured using the metre stick.

Ask some children to stand in a line. Ask others how long they estimate the line of children to be, in metres.

Estimate other long distances in the school. Children can practise estimation in groups of four. Put four cards marked 1 m, 2 m, 3 m, 4 m in a box. Each child picks a card. They then go into the playground or corridor and estimate the length of their distances using chalk marks. Lengths can then be measured using a tape measure or long tape measure.

WHO MADE THE MOST ACCURATE ESTIMATE?

Turn this activity into a game by giving the child with the most accurate estimate a point. The activity can be repeated several times to find a 'winner'.

5 Using a cm tape and a metre stick

Talk with the children about measuring distances between 1 m and 2 m. Explain that they can use the metre stick first and then measure the extra distance with a tape measure marked in cm. They might use this technique to measure their heights as in Section B of the pupils' book. When children measure how high they can reach, they can make a mark on the wall or board with a piece of chalk. They can then measure down from the mark using a metre stick, then measure the extra cm with a tape measure.

6 Rounding to the nearest metre

Talk about rounding to the nearest metre. Ask the children to estimate their height or the height of an adult to the nearest metre.

7 The metre and centimetre tape

Show the chlidren a long tape measure marked in metres and centimetres and talk about how to use it to record measurements accurately.

8 The trundle wheel

Can the children suggest ways of measuring longer distances? Talk about the problems of measuring longer distances with tape measures and how it is easier to use a trundle wheel if we want to find a distance in metres.

Let the children measure the corridor with a trundle wheel. Do they always get the same answer? If not, why not? Talk about the position of the first 'click' on a trundle wheel.

Let the children estimate and measure other long distances, such as the length of or distance round the hall and compare their results. Let them sketch a plan and enter the measurements.

9 Measuring in PE

There are ideal opportunities for measuring in games and PE lessons. Let the children decide which measures to use. Should they measure in cm or m? Do they want to use a tape measure, metre stick or a trundle wheel? Wherever possible, let them estimate first.

- How far can they flick a bean bag with their foot?
- How many metres can they throw a ball?
- Who can make the longest hop?
- How high can they jump?

Measure tracks for team races.
Have a mini Olympics. For example, hold Pentathlon events.

10 The mile

Although it is not part of the metric system, many children will be familiar with measuring longer distances in miles.

Talk about why we still use the mile as a standard unit of measurement. Ask them to estimate a distance of 1 mile from school.

Where do they see distances written in miles?

LINKS WITH THE ENVIRONMENT

- Talk about how we need our measurements when we shop for clothes and shoes. How do shops show measurements and sizes?
- How are feet measured for shoes in shops?
- Have the children ever seen material measured using a metal rod or measure fixed to a counter?
- Wood is often measured on a cutting machine in a DIY shop.
- Look at labels on clothes and make a collection.

- Look at knitting and sewing patterns and read the measurements.
- Compare children's achievements in running and jumping with Olympic records. Mark out the distances and compare them.
- Talk about the lengths of the different races in the Olympics.
- Swimming certificates. Shorter distances are usually measured in metres. Some awards still give longer distances in miles.
- Estimate the length of familiar objects in metres, for example, cars and buses.
- When are trundle wheels used? Have the children seen a wheel being used perhaps in connection with road works?

NOTES ON INVESTIGATIONS

Section A

Talk to the children about this activity. Do they realise which measurements they need for the clothes they choose? For example, a skirt needs a waist and length measurement.

Do they ask a friend to help them find the measurements? Do they record them in a sensible way?

Section B

Are the children able to measure their friend's left foot accurately, for example, by placing the heel against the wall?

Do they make a record of the foot and shoe sizes of their friends so that they can compare the results?

Do they discover that most children with similar length feet wear shoes of the same size? If not, why not? Talk about shoes that are slightly too large or too small.

Talk about continental sizes.

What size are their shoes? Do all shoes of the same size look the same? Shoe designs vary and boys' shoes may look bigger than girls' shoes of the same size.

Section C

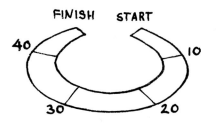

Do the children first see if they can fit a 50 m track across the length or width of the playground? Do they go about the task in a logical way such as making a mark or placing a skittle at the beginning and the end?

Do they appreciate that a track may be circular or oval? Do they realise that they will then have to mark out more than just the start and the finish?

Do they ask another person to check their track?

Do they do the same for 100 m? Do they realise that, for 100 m, they can go round a shorter track several times, for example, twice round the 50 m track?

Weight 1

Purpose

- To add and subtract grams
- To estimate weight
- To give practice in weighing activities

Materials

Balance scales, weights (up to 500 g), bag of cubes for weighing

Vocabulary

Total, weight, weigh, weighs, answer, estimate, order, lighter, lightest, heavier, heaviest, ingredient, different, recipe, contents

TEACHING POINTS

1 Appreciating weight

Talk with the children about carrying heavy things such as shopping, library books, sports equipment, school stock, school bag, holiday luggage.

2 Grams and kilograms

Talk about weighing objects such as boxes and model building bricks using gram weights. Explain that heavier things, such as people, may find their weights in kilograms. Do the children know their weights in kilograms?

3 Estimating

Let the children estimate the weights of items that they often carry, for example, a lunch box, a sports bag, a school bag containing two library books. Allow them to check their estimates by weighing. Let them estimate the weight of their jacket, shoes, jumper, etc.

It is interesting to think about the total weights we carry at different times. Bring in some typical groceries in a shopping bag and let the children estimate the total weight. Then let them weigh the bag to find the total weight. Ask them to describe what they have done.
'How near was your estimate?'
'Was the total more than 1 kg?' (Revise that 1000g = 1 kg.)

Why is a holiday suitcase heavy? Consider all the things that are packed in it (don't forget the weight of the case itself). Weigh some clothes. Weigh the case. When is the weight of suitcases important?

A game to play

ESTIMATE THE WEIGHT

This game can be played in teams. Each team in turn estimates the weight of an object selected by the teacher. The object is then weighed by the children. A correct estimate (within limits set by teacher) wins a point for the team. The winning team has most points after six objects have been used.

4 Addition of grams

Talk about adding weights. Show the children that adding grams is like adding hundreds, tens and units.

$$
\begin{array}{r}
\text{g} \\
246 \\
+\ 147 \\
\hline
 \\
\hline
\end{array}
$$

5 Subtraction of grams

Talk about times when we might subtract weight. For example, if we have 250 g of margarine and use 125 g, how much is left?

Show the children that we can set down the subtraction like hundreds, tens and units.

$$
\begin{array}{r}
\text{g} \\
250 \\
-\ 125 \\
\hline
 \\
\hline
\end{array}
$$

6 Mental work

Encourage the children to add and subtract weights mentally, for example, 100 g + 20 g, 200 g − 50 g.

Can they think of easy ways to add? For example,

250 g + 125 g = (200 g + 100 g) + (50 g + 25 g) = 300 g + 75 g = 375 g

A variation is for the teacher to add the weights:
'I am holding two weights. They make 200 g. What might they be?'

7 Ounces, pounds and stones

Although not part of the metric system, many children may be familiar with weight being stated in ounces, pounds and stones. Discuss this and ask for instances when non-metric weights are used; for example, some food packets and recipes still show weights in pounds and ounces. In the USA people give their weight in pounds.

USING THE CALCULATOR

Let the children use the calculator to check some of their answers.

Show typical grocery items. Let the children look at the labels and choose the ones often bought by their family. Then let them add the total weight.

Let the children work out the total weight of, for example, beans they eat in a week (by checking the weight on the can).

LINKS WITH THE ENVIRONMENT

Talk about times when we use weight in everyday life.

- Cooking – weights in recipes. Let the children weigh and make cakes in school (a cooker is not always necessary).
- Shopping. Look at weight labels on food items as some are still marked in pounds.
- Luggage. When is there a weight limit on luggage? Luggage is weighed at airports to calculate the fuel needed for the journey.
- Shelves and bridges. Why do some things have a 'maximum weight' sign?
- Sweets. Pick'n'Mix situations.
- Animal food. How much does your pet eat? A calculator may be needed to help work this out.
- Lunch time. What weight of food is in a lunch box?

NOTES ON INVESTIGATIONS

Section A

Do the children make reasonable estimates?

Do they use one result to help with another? For example, if they are close with estimating 50 g of cubes, do they double up to make the 100 g set?

Section B

Do the children realise that, initially, this is a subtraction situation?

Do they then appreciate that the 310 g may be split up in a variety of ways? For example,

100 g + 100 g + 110 g
100 g + 101 g + 109 g
100 g + 102 g + 108 g

Do they give realistic answers, and not make a slice of pie 1 g?

Section C

Do the children find a way, initially, for making the weights two and a half times greater? Or do they find, for example, the weight for one person and then multiply by 5?

Capacity 1

Purpose

- To introduce the millilitre
- To introduce addition and subtraction of millilitres
- To give practice in pouring activities
- To give practice in problem situations

Materials

Litre, 500 ml and 100 ml measuring jugs, selection of drink containers including litre, 750 ml and 250 ml bottles, mug, beaker, large plastic ice-cream tub, cup, yogurt pot, water, 1 litre orange squash bottle, funnel

Vocabulary

Litre (l), millilitre (ml), half litre jug, full, estimate, bottle, pour, poured, pouring, hole, water mark, measure, difference between, ingredient, recipe, punch

TEACHING POINTS

1 Litres

Talk about things which come in litres, such as milk, soft drinks, petrol, paint, classroom glue. Some everyday drinks still come in pints but explain that people in Britain are slowly changing to the metric system.

Look at and talk about the different shaped litre bottles or containers. Remind the children how to record the litre as l.

2 Millilitres

Ask the children if they ever have drinks from containers smaller than a litre. Talk about the capacities of these smaller containers, for example, 250 ml small bottles, 330 ml cans.

Talk about the millilitre as a unit of measurement. Explain that 1000 millilitres (ml) equals 1 litre (l). Mention that the word 'milli' means thousandth.

3 Measuring jugs

Talk with the children about measuring liquids using measuring jugs, and explain that there are different sizes of these.

Give the children experience in filling containers up to given marks.

4 Pouring acitivities

Give the children practical pouring activities. Ask them to predict whether the contents of a tall jug or cylinder will fill one with a different size of base. Get them to check to see if they were right. Ask them to describe what happens.

Does a litre bottle really hold a litre? Let the children check this by filling a litre measure then pouring it into the bottle using a funnel. Ask if the bottle is full to the very top. If it not, why not? Ask the children to mark where the litre of liquid comes up to.

The children might like to find out how much an empty small drink-carton holds.

5 Estimating and measuring activity

Collect different sizes of containers. Ask the children to estimate how much they hold and arrange them in order of estimated capacity.

Let them then measure the capacity of each and label them. Do they now have to change the order?

Are there any containers that will hold more than 1 litre? Ask the children to estimate first then measure.

6 Addition of millilitres

Talk about times when we might need to add millilitres. For example, if a teacher wants to know how much glue is in the stock room we can add the 500 ml and 250 ml bottles.

If we make jelly, we add 300 ml of hot water and then 150 ml of cold water. How much water is added altogether?

Explain how we add millilitres in a similar way to hundreds, tens and units.

$$
\begin{array}{r}
\text{ml} \\
300 \\
+\ \underline{150} \\
\overline{}
\end{array}
$$

7 Subtraction of millilitres

If we need to find the difference between capacities we can subtract. Explain that the subtraction of millilitres is recorded in a similar way to hundreds, tens and units.

$$
\begin{array}{r}
\text{ml} \\
350 \\
- \ \underline{100} \\
\hline
\end{array}
$$

8 A game to play

Put out a collection of containers with capacities of 1 litre or less, for example, perfume bottles, medicine bottles, vases, plastic bottles, beakers and jugs. Measure their capacity beforehand and make labels for each. Give a group of children the labels; they have to try, by estimating, to match each label with its container. Then they measure the capacity of each container to see if they were correct. Each correct estimate scores one point. The children then give the labels to another group to see if they can score more.

9 Mental work

Ask the children to count up to 1000 in 100's, 200's, 50's, etc. Can they count back in 200's from 1000?

USING THE CALCULATOR   *A game to play*

MAKE A LITRE

Mark 10 cards in millilitres. Give two children a calculator each, and deal a card to each. They enter the millilitres onto their calculator. Another card is dealt to each, and the children add that to the first number. They continue to do this until they reach 1000 ml or as near as possible to it.

If they go over 1 litre they have lost. The winner is the one who makes 1 litre exactly or is the nearest to it.

LINKS WITH THE ENVIRONMENT

- Talk with the children about the capacity labels in shops. Make a list of which containers hold more than a litre and which hold less.
- Make a collection of pictures of containers marked in millilitres, using catalogues, posters and advertising brochures.
- Petrol is bought in litres. How many litres does it take to fill a petrol tank? Cars vary in the capacities of their tanks.
- Perfume is sold in small bottles, for example $7\frac{1}{2}$ ml. Why are the quantities so small?
- Paint is usually sold in litres. Why is this?
- Recipes sometimes use millilitres. Collect recipes which use metric capacities.
- Music – measure different millilitre amounts of water and put them in jam jars. Put them in order and strike them to make notes and tunes.
- Rainfall can be collected and measured. This is often measured in millilitres. Compare rainfall in this country and in countries abroad. Where does a great deal of rain fall?

NOTES ON INVESTIGATIONS

Section A

Do the children suggest filling the container with 1 litre of water? Do they realise that if there is 1 litre in the container, the hole must be just above the 1 litre level or else the water will flow out? Can they explain what they would do and why?

Section B

Do the children realise that $\frac{1}{2}$ litre is 500 ml? Do they use all four types of drinks in their recipe? Do they try to get the same balance of ingredients as in the recipe in the book? Does the total of the ingredients add up to 500 ml?

Section C

How do the children attempt this investigation? Do they first check the number of children in the class? Do they use the information in questions 1 and 2? Do they work it out by pencil and paper methods or with a calculator? Do they find out using pouring activities? Are they able to work out how many bottles of squash they would need to make drinks for the whole class?

Time 1

Purpose

- To introduce five minute intervals, including digital notation
- To introduce 'minutes to' and 'minutes past' in five minute intervals

Materials

Clock stamp, clock faces would be an advantage

Vocabulary

Minutes past, minutes to, clock face, times, clock, digital times, o'clock, half past, departure time, arrival, quarter past, quarter to

TEACHING POINTS

1 Clocks and watches

Ask the children about the clocks and watches we see and use.
'Who has a watch? What kind is it? Is it digital or one with a face?'
'What are the numbers on a clock face?'
'What are the names for the hands?' – hour, minute.
    Remind the children that the long hand is the minute hand and the short hand shows the hour.

2 Revise o'clock, half past, quarter past, quarter to

Use a real clock or geared clock face. Set the hands to o'clock times, for example, 7 o'clock, 9 o'clock. Ask what time is shown.
    Repeat this with the hands set to half past, quarter past and quarter to.
    Talk about the time of particular happenings at school, such as playtime, lunchtime, time for PE.
    Talk about the movement of a clock's hands and show half past, quarter past, quarter to as fractions of a circle.

    Draw some clock faces on the blackboard with the times written underneath. Ask the children to draw in the hands.

half past 7
$\frac{1}{2}$ past 7
7:30

3 Revise digital notation for o'clock and half past

Remind the children that digital watches and clocks show the time in numbers only. Talk about which numbers show the hour and which show the minutes.

Remind them that there are 60 minutes in an hour, and talk about the various ways of recording the time, for example, half past 7, $\frac{1}{2}$ past 7, 7:30.

Ask the children to draw or stamp some clock faces in their books and record the times in various ways.

4 Introduce five minute intervals

Ask the children to count in fives up to 60, and show these five minute intervals on the clock face. Ask the children to join the following numbers on a clock face: 12–6, 1–7, 2–8, 3–9, 4–10, 5–11. These divide the clock into 5 minute intervals.

Use this to ask how many minutes the long hand passes through when it moves from 12 to 3 ($5 + 5 + 5 = 15$ minutes).
'How many minutes does the long hand pass through when it moves from 4 to 8?' ($5 + 5 + 5 + 5 = 20$ minutes).

5 Estimating

Ask the children to estimate what they can do in five minutes; for example, run round the field, walk to the shops, do five lines of a story, do a spelling test. Make a list of five minute jobs or activities in the classroom.

6 Five minute intervals past the hour

Talk about five minute intervals past the hour. Draw the numbers, 0, 5, 10, 15, 20, 25, . . . around the clock face.

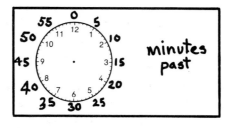

Set the hands to various times. Talk about the times shown and the method of recording.

10 minutes past 4

7 Five minute intervals to the hour

Draw a clock face. Put the numbers 0, 5, 10, 15, 20, 25, 30, 25, 20, 15, 10, 5 around it. Talk about counting time to the next hour in five minute intervals.

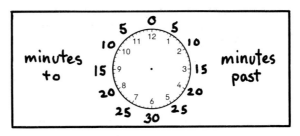

Set the hands to various times and talk about the method of recording.

20 minutes to 1

A game to play

MINUTES TO, MINUTES PAST

Make two different coloured circles of card of different sizes and cut them to their centres. Number one circle 1 to 12, and divide the other into five minute intervals. Slot one inside the other to make one clock face.

Put the children into groups or teams. Ask one person from each team to set the clock. A member from the other team has to say how many minutes 'past' or 'to' the clock shows. They score 1 point for each correct answer. In this example either 'twenty minutes to' or 'forty minutes past' is acceptable and scores one point.

The winning team is the one with the highest score at the end of the game.

The game could be varied to use just 'minutes past' or 'minutes to'.

8 Digital notation for five minute intervals

Talk about how to write digital times. Explain that 5 minutes past 10 is written 10:05, so that the minute numbers must always be recorded as two numbers. The hour numbers are usually recorded as one or two numbers where appropriate, for example 7:25, 12:05.

Remind the children that quarter past 1 is written as 1:15 and quarter to 2 as 1:45.

Hold up a clock face with the hands set at a particular time. Ask the children to say the time in different ways, such as 20 minutes to 4, 40 minutes past 3, 3:40.

Ask the children to draw some clock faces in their books and show the times in different ways.

A game to play

TRIOS

You need a set of 36 cards made up in 'trios' like this.

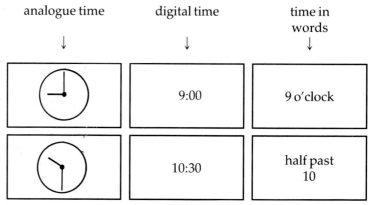

analogue time	digital time	time in words
(clock showing 9:00)	9:00	9 o'clock
(clock showing 10:30)	10:30	half past 10

The game is for 2 to 4 players.

- Each player is dealt 6 cards from the shuffled pack.
- The remaining cards are placed face down, with the top card turned over.
- Players sort their cards aiming to make 'trios' of matching times. Any trios made are placed face up in front of the player.
- The first player takes either the upturned card or one from the top of the pile. This card can be kept if required to make a trio, or replaced face up. If the card is kept, one other card must be placed face up on the pile.
- Players take turns like this, making trios where possible.
- When all the cards are used, the pack can be shuffled for play to continue.
- The game can end after a specified time, or when all the trios have been made.
- The winner is the one with the most trios.

The game can be varied by using only o'clock or half past or by using 5 minute intervals.

9 Mental work

Ask the children to work out mentally the answers to questions like these.

- What is the next number in the fives pattern 5, 10, 15, 20, 25?
- How many minutes past the hour is it if the minute hand points to 11?
- How many minutes to the hour is it if the minute hand points to 7?
- What will the time be 10 minutes after 1 o'clock?
- What will the time be $\frac{1}{2}$ an hour after 5:50?

USING THE CALCULATOR

The constant function on the calculator may be used to count five minute intervals, from 0 up to 60.

Talk about the pattern of fives. Numbers on the clock face could be multiplied by 5 to find the number of minutes past the hour.

$9 \times 5 = \square$

LINKS WITH THE ENVIRONMENT

Talk about the type of clocks and watches we see in everyday life. Which have faces and which are digital? Where do we see clocks?

- At home – alarm clocks, cooker clocks, grandfather clock, watch, videos.
- On the way to school – church clock, clocks and watches in a jeweller's shop window, bus station, railway station.
- At school – classroom clock, school clock, children's watches.
- Make a display of clocks and watches or pictures from catalogues. Look at the many different faces and sizes.
- Talk about things which are commonly measured in hours, minutes and seconds. For example, journeys (hours), cooking (minutes), 100 metre race (seconds).

NOTES ON INVESTIGATIONS

Section A

Do the children appreciate why we need to know the times for different things at school like assembly, playtime, dinner time, TV programmes or PE lessons?

Do the children appreciate that things like whistles blowing, bells ringing, dinner tables being set or parents waiting outside school all happen at different times in the school day?

Section B

Do the children write the digital time correctly, using two digits for the minutes? Do they try to find all the possibilities?

5:00, 5:05, 0:55, 0:50, 5:55, 0:00.

Do any of the children write 05:05, 00:55, 05:50 or 00:00? These are acceptable answers since railway timetables are recorded in this way.

Do any of the children write incorrect times? For example, 55:00, 55:50 or 55:55?

Section C

Do the children's digital times show 25 minute intervals? Are the hours different?

Do they start with an o'clock time first, for example, 11:00 and 10:35? Are they systematic in showing other times? For example 11:05 and 10:40, 11:10 and 10:45, etc.

Do they record the digital times correctly?

Angles 1

Purpose

- To revise right angles
- To introduce the four points of the compass (N, S, E, W)
- To develop children's sense of direction
- To introduce 90° and 180°

Materials

Cardboard, paper fastener, cm squared paper, map of Britain, map of the world, compass

Vocabulary

North, south, east, west, faces, turns, clockwise, right angle, square corner, compass, directions, turtle, plan

TEACHING POINTS

1 Right angles

Revise the right angle or square corner and let the children make one by folding paper. Mark the right angle on the square corner.

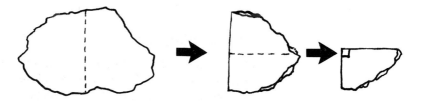

Show the children a set square and point out the right angle. How can the paper right angle (or set square) be used for finding a right angle?

Look for right angles around the room.

90° and 180°

Talk with the children about degrees. They might be interested in the story of a possible origin of the number of degrees in a circle, when through studying the stars and changing seasons, people thought that the cycle of the year was 360 days. They divided the cycle (or circle) into 360 degrees, each to represent one day.

A quarter of a complete circle is 90° or a right angle. Half of a complete circle is 180° or 2 right angles.

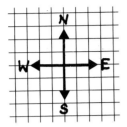

2 Compass points

Talk about walking through a town or city. There are signs to show the way. But how do walkers in the hills or sailors at sea find their way?

Show the children a simple compass and explain its use. Talk about the four points of the compass and explain how they may be written as N, S, E, W.

Draw them on a sheet of squared paper. Let children see that there is a right angle or 90° between each point as you move around the compass.

3 Class compass

Discuss with the children how to make a large class compass. Make a pointer for it and use a paper fastener to attach it.

Let the children use it to count how many right angles there are between different points of the compass. For example, if you start at south and move clockwise (revise this) through 2 right angles or 180°, where do you finish?

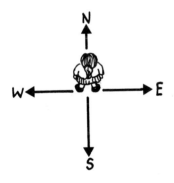

4 Floor compass

Use a compass to find N, S, E, W, in the classroom. If possible, mark the four points on the floor.

Ask a child to stand in the middle of the room, face north and turn through 90° clockwise. Where is she facing now?

5 Turtle or big track

One excellent use of the floor turtle or big track is to demonstrate turning movement. This is an enjoyable way for children to become familiar with turning in different directions. Use either verbal instructions, or write them on card, for children to practise.
'The Turtle is facing north.'
'If it turns 90° anticlockwise, which direction will it face?'
If there is no turtle or big track available, the activity can still be enjoyed using the children themselves. Make a turtle mask, and choose one child to be the turtle. Another child, or a small group, give the turtle directions, and say where the turtle faces.

6 Playground compass

Mark the four points of the compass in the playground. Play similar activities to those in the classroom.

Look at the position of familiar features around the school and its surroundings. Work out their directions from the school.

7 Direction

Talk to the children about direction. What do we do when we 'follow directions'?

Talk about directions from the school. For example,
'We have to go to the north to reach the paper shop.'
'If we go south we come to the park.'
'What do we see when we face east?'

8 Following directions

Ask the children to move around the classroom in given directions – 1 step north, 3 steps to the east, and so on.

This may also be done with a floor turtle if the school has one. For example,

```
FORWARD  20
RIGHT     90
FORWARD  20
```

A game to play

This is best played in pairs or small groups. One child is the 'turtle'.

The turtle places an object somewhere on the floor and then stands elsewhere facing away from the object. The partner, or group, gives instructions for the turtle to get to the object using 'degrees', 'clockwise', 'anticlockwise', 'north', 'south', 'east', 'west', 'forward' and 'stop'. The aim is to get the turtle to the object as quickly as possible.

At first the game is best played in an open space with no obstacles. Then varying numbers of obstacles can be introduced so that more complex instructions are needed.

Draw a large squared grid on the blackboard or on a large piece of paper. Mark the four points of the compass. Show the children how to follow routes using N, S, E, W.

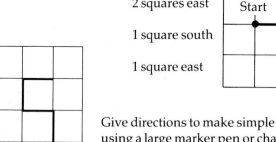

2 squares east

1 square south

1 square east

Give directions to make simple shapes or letters on the squared paper, using a large marker pen or chalk.

Let the children plan simple shapes and give directions for others to draw them.

9 Positions on plans and maps

Draw a simple plan of the classroom for class use. Discuss the positions of particular objects. For example, the book corner is at the south end of the room.

Consider the position of the children in relation to their friends. For example, who sits to the east of Jane?

Games to play

- Put the four compass points up in the hall. Call out a compass point and the children run or turn to it. The last one is out.
- One child calls directions: 'Face south'. 'Simon says: turn 2 right angles clockwise'.
  An easier version is 'Face east', 'Face north'.
- Play a direction-finding game in the yard:
  'Stand in the middle.'
  'Walk to the east side of the yard.'
- Make a simple treasure hunt. Write it out for children to follow.
  1 Go south to the tree
  2 Turn and go west to the fence
  . . . .
- Let children work out a simple route around the school. A friend has to follow it. Where do they finish up?

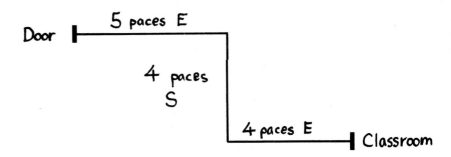

- There are lots of opportunities for plans and map work in school: plan direction routes round the school and grounds or build up a picture map of the school surroundings.
- Direction and map work: Which are the most northern and southern points in the world? Where does the sun set and rise? Does the weather change when you go north or south? In which direction do birds migrate? Do maps show compass points? Look at a local map – which places are N, S, E or W of school? Look at a map of the British Isles – which places are in the north, south, east or west?

NOTES ON
INVESTIGATIONS

Section A

Do the children move correctly along the lines of the squares, counting carefully as they go?

Do they state the directions and do these correspond with the drawings they make on squared paper?

Section B

Do the children fix a starting point to begin with? Do they attempt to draw some interesting plans of their own? Do the directions they give correspond with their drawings, that is, do they give accurate directions?

This activity can be extended to producing simple plans on squared paper.

Section C

Can the children find the British Isles on the world map? Are they accurate in finding countries to the N, S, E or W of the British Isles?

Do they make a sensible choice of another country and find one that gives them sufficient choice for north, south, east and west?

This activity may be extended to planning world trips in particular directions.

Children could write stories about magic carpets etc. – 'The magic carpet left England, and travelled west to New York and then headed south to the Caribbean . . .'

Number 6

Purpose

- To give practice in HTU place value
- To give practice in the addition of hundreds, tens and units with 'carrying' from the units and tens
- To identify patterns in addition

Materials

Squared paper, calculators, 100 square, number cards

Vocabulary

Score, pattern, odd, numbers (in words), highest possible score

TEACHING POINTS

1 Find a pattern

Talk about looking for patterns in numbers. Relate this to house numbers and revise odd and even numbers on doors. For example,

1   3   5   7   9   . . .
2   4   6   8   10   . . .

Explain that we know what the next numbers are because we recognise the pattern.

Talk with the children about number patterns they see as they walk to school. Do they see car numbers with patterns?

F   2   4   6   A   R   W

2 Games to play

MAKE THE PATTERN

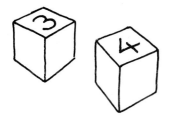

Throw a die numbered 1–6. The score gives the starting number. Throw the die again. The score gives the addition number. The children have to write down the first five numbers in the sequence. (A 100 square might be useful.)

3 (+ 4) 7 (+ 4) 11 (+ 4) 15 (+ 4) 19

MISSING HOUSES

This is a variation on the previous game. Children pretend they are standing in a street on the 'odd' or 'even' side and at the first house numbered 1 or 2. The die score gives the number of houses to be missed out each time. The children have then to write three numbers, allowing for the missing houses each time.

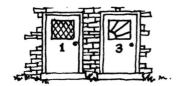

Starting at 1. Die score is 3.

1   (3   5   7)   9   (11   13   15)   17

Starting at 2. Die score is 5.

2   (4   6   8   10   12)   14   (16   18   20   22   24)   26

3 Place value of HTU

Talk with the children about place value. Remind them that 457 is 400 + 50 + 7. If necessary, use number cards to show this:

400   50   7   →   4 5 7

Remind them how to record HTU using a spike abacus or dotted pictures.

Give the children practice in expanding numbers and adding again. For example,

$$652 \rightarrow 600 + 50 + 2 \quad \text{and}$$

$$\begin{array}{r} 600 \\ 50 \\ + 2 \\ \hline 652 \end{array}$$

4 Addition

Use structural apparatus to show addition of HTU and 'carrying' from the tens and units.

```
H T U
2 7 5
+ 1 4 6
———
```

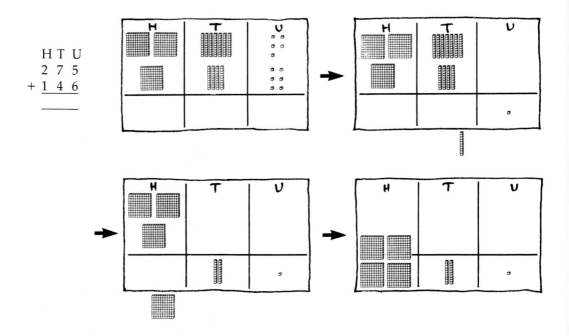

Keep your usual form of words and method of recording.

5 Mental work

Use activities like these to help children readily manipulate numbers.
- Give the next number in this sequence: 3, 6, 9. Can children identify the pattern (adding 3)?
- Quick addition of number bonds, for example, $3 + 7$, $16 + 4$, $27 + 3$. Revise the quick method for adding 9.
- Bridging the tens, $9 + 4$, $19 + 4$, $29 + 4$.

USING THE CALCULATOR

Revise how to switch on and enter three-digit numbers.

Let the children practise sums, for example, 275 + 146. Talk about estimating the answer. For example, 275 is close to 300 so the answer is four hundred and something.

Use the constant function to add on numbers to show number patterns. Pick different starting numbers.

Add 5

243   248   253   258   263   268

Add 6

246   252   258   264   270   276   282   288

Talk about the pattern in the last digit.

A game to play

Two players use one calculator. The first player writes down two three-digit numbers to be added like 278 and 465. The second player then has to estimate the answer to the nearest hundred. Do they think the true answer will be more or less?

The first player then uses the calculator to check.

The players then change over.

LINKS WITH THE ENVIRONMENT

- Look for number patterns in the environment. For example, the pattern of house numbers, or the pattern for numbering players in a football team.
- Look for patterns in three-digit numbers, in car numbers or on houses; for example, 246, 369, 842 etc. Encourage children to discover new patterns. This can be done over a period of time and the patterns collected and displayed.
- Look for times when we add three-digit numbers. For example, the two innings of a cricket match.

NOTES ON INVESTIGATIONS

Section A

Do the children realise that the easiest way is to start at 120 and count back? Do they use a system to structure their patterns by counting, for example, in ones, then twos, then threes, . . . ?

Section B

Do the children devise a strategy for collecting ducks or make random choices? Do they, for example, use a calculator to divide 120 by the number of ducks and then look for the required number of ducks showing that number? For example,

$120 \div 3$ (ducks) = 40.   Collect three ducks marked 40.

Do they then look for other ways? For example,

$40 + 40 + 40$

$50 + 30 + 40$

$60 + 20 + 40$ etc.

Section C

Do the children adopt a system for making up patterns? Do they, for example, devise a system where they add 1, then 2, then 3, etc.?

Purpose

- To develop awareness of number patterns
- To introduce subtraction of HTU with decomposition from the hundreds

Materials

Structural apparatus as required

Vocabulary

Score, starts, total, odd, different, subtract, finish, finishing, starting number, numbering

TEACHING POINTS   **1 Patterns**

Talk with the children about number patterns and how numbers can make patterns. Use different forms of the 100 square and colour in patterns.

Talk about addition patterns. Ask the children to count on aloud, or write the pattern. For example,

0	1	2	3	4	5	6	7	8	9
10	11	12	13	14	15	16	17	18	19
20	21	22	23	24	25	26	27	28	29
30	31	32	33	34	35	36	37	38	39
40	41	42	43	44	45	46	47	48	49
50	51	52	53	54	55	56	57	58	59
60	61	62	63	64	65	66	67	68	69
70	71	72	73	74	75	76	77	78	79
80	81	82	83	84	85	86	87	88	89
90	91	92	93	94	95	96	97	98	99

1	2	3	4	5	6	7	8	9	10
11	12	13	14	15	16	17	18	19	20
21	22	23	24	25	26	27	28	29	30
31	32	33	34	35	36	37	38	39	40
41	42	43	44	45	46	47	48	49	50
51	52	53	54	55	56	57	58	59	60
61	62	63	64	65	66	67	68	69	70
71	72	73	74	75	76	77	78	79	80
81	82	83	84	85	86	87	88	89	90
91	92	93	94	95	96	97	98	99	100

100	99	98	97	96	95	94	93	92	91
81	82	83	84	85	86	87	88	89	90
80	79	78	77	76	75	74	73	72	71
61	62	63	64	65	66	67	68	69	70
60	59	58	57	56	55	54	53	52	51
41	42	43	44	45	46	47	48	49	50
40	39	38	37	36	35	34	33	32	31
21	22	23	24	25	26	27	28	29	30
20	19	18	17	16	15	14	13	12	11
1	2	3	4	5	6	7	8	9	10

- Start at 10. Count in ones to 25.   10, 11, 12, . . . , 25
- Start at 23. Count in twos to 39.   23, 25, 27, . . . , 39
- Start at 5. Count in fives to 50.   5, 10, 15, . . . , 50
- Start at 13. Count in tens to 193.   13, 23, 33, . . . , 193
- Start at 107. Count in hundreds to 907.   107, 207, 307, ..., 907

Talk about subtraction patterns. Ask the children to count down or subtract. For example,

- Count down in ones from 25   25, 24, 23, . . . , 0
- Count down in twos from 20.   20, 18, 16, . . . , 0
- Count down in fives from 40.   40, 35, 30, . . . , 0
- Count down in tens from 100.   100, 90, 80, . . . , 0
- Count down in twenties from 100.   100, 80, 60, . . . , 0
- Count down in hundreds from 900.   900, 800, 700, . . . , 0

2 Revise subtraction of HTU, including decomposition from the tens

Talk with the children about vertical recording of subtraction. Use structural apparatus to show it.

$$
\begin{array}{r}
\text{H T U} \\
2\ 5\ 3 \\
-\ \ \ 2\ 8 \\
\hline
\end{array}
$$

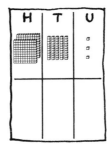
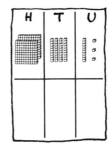
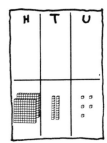

Talk about methods of recording this. Here is one example.

$$
\begin{array}{r}
\text{H T U} \\
2\ 5\ 3 \\
-\ \ \ 2\ 8 \\
\hline
\end{array}
\quad\rightarrow\quad
\begin{array}{r}
\text{H T U} \\
2\ ^4 5\ ^1 3 \\
-\ \ \ 2\ 8 \\
\hline
\end{array}
\quad\rightarrow\quad
\begin{array}{r}
\text{H T U} \\
2\ ^4 5\ ^1 3 \\
-\ \ \ 2\ 8 \\
\hline
2\ 2\ 5
\end{array}
$$

It is best to use your own words and methods, but the important point is to give the children the imagery for the mathematics.

3 Subtraction of HTU with decomposition from the hundreds

Talk with the children about decomposition from the hundreds. Again use your own words and methods to explain what is happening. Here is one way of using structural apparatus to show it.

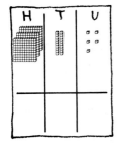 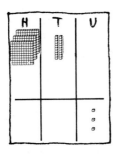 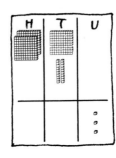 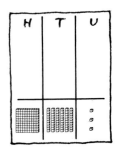

$$
\begin{array}{cccc}
\begin{array}{c} \text{H T U} \\ 3\ 2\ 5 \\ -\ 1\ 6\ 2 \\ \hline \end{array}
&
\begin{array}{c} \text{H T U} \\ 3\ 2\ 5 \\ -\ 1\ 6\ 2 \\ \hline 3 \end{array}
&
\begin{array}{c} \text{H T U} \\ {}^{2}3\ {}^{1}2\ 5 \\ -\ 1\ 6\ 2 \\ \hline 3 \end{array}
&
\begin{array}{c} \text{H T U} \\ {}^{2}3\ {}^{1}2\ 5 \\ -\ 1\ 6\ 2 \\ \hline 1\ 6\ 3 \end{array}
\end{array}
$$

Talk about different methods of recording this. Have the children developed any of their own ways for recording?

4 Horizontal to vertical recording

Talk with the children about horizontal to vertical recording. For example,

$$
423 - 131 \rightarrow \begin{array}{r} 423 \\ -\ 131 \\ \hline \end{array}
$$

It is important that they think about the place value of the numbers.

5 Mental work

Ask the children various questions to do mentally. Get the children to make up their own mental questions. Give them examples such as these.
'Find the next number in the pattern 3, 6, 9, 12.'
'What is the next number in this pattern? 43, 42, 41, 40'.
'Add the numbers 57 and 4.'
'Add 10, 10, 5.'
'Add 9 + 9 + 9 (by adding 10 and subtracting 1 each time).'

'Find the total of 20, 20, 20.'
'Take 1 away from 90.'
'Find the difference between 23 and 15.'
'What is the answer to this? 20, take away 1, take away 1, take away 2.'

USING THE CALCULATOR

Remind the children how to use the constant function on the calculator to find addition and subtraction patterns. For example, 907, 807, 707, 607, 507, 407, 307, 207, 107.

Use the patterns to reinforce place value. For example,

Start at 103. Count in ones to 120.   103, 104, 105, 106, 107, 108, 109, 110, . . . , 120

Beware of some children writing 1010 for 110 if they are not using a calculator.

Give the children subtraction practice using the calculator.

A game to play

GUESS THE NUMBER

Two players use one calculator. Both players write a three-digit number on a piece of paper. For example, 425 and 294. Both children estimate or guess in 10 seconds the difference between the two numbers. They take turns to use the calculator to find the answer. The nearest estimate or guess scores 1 point. An accurate estimate scores 2 points. The winner is the first player to score 20 points.

LINKS WITH THE ENVIRONMENT

Talk about where we might meet subtraction situations involving large numbers in everyday life. These might include:

- Subtracting from 301 or 501 in a game of darts
- The number of days left to the end of term

NOTES ON INVESTIGATIONS

Section A

Do the children's ski runs have 243 at the start and 220 at the finish? Do they have 3 flags? Do the children's flags add up to 23 each time?

Do any of the children start at 220 and add 20, then 2, then 1, or 10, 10 and 3? Do they use number patterns to find alternative answers?

For example,

10	10	3	or	1	1	21
10	9	4		1	2	20
10	8	5		1	3	19
10	7	6 etc.		1	4	18 etc.

The investigation could be extended by changing the scores at the start and finish of the ski run.

Section B

Do the children appreciate that the difference between the starting and finishing numbers is 189 (i.e. 100 + 80 + 9 on the flags)? Are they systematic in finding different scores for starting and finishing? For example,

$$290 - 189 = 101$$
$$291 - 189 = 102$$
$$292 - 189 = 103$$
$$293 - 189 = 104$$
$$294 - 189 = 105$$
$$295 - 189 = 106$$
$$296 - 189 = 107$$
$$297 - 189 = 108$$
$$298 - 189 = 109$$

Do the children still remember that the starting number in the ski run must be larger than the finishing number?

This investigation could be extended by changing the three numbers in the flags or the range for the starting and finishing numbers.

Section C

Are the children systematic in finding three odd numbers that add up to 67? For example,

1	3	63
1	5	61
1	7	59 etc.

Do the children appreciate that odd + odd + odd = odd?

shape 2

Purpose

- To identify shapes that tessellate
- To identify shapes that do not tessellate

Materials

Templates, squares, circles, squared paper, equilateral triangles, hexagons, pentagons

Vocabulary

Tessellate, tessellation, square, circle, rectangle, equilateral triangle, hexagon, pentagon, shape

TEACHING POINTS

1 What is a tessellation?

Talk about tessellating shapes that fit together without overlapping or leaving gaps. Discuss examples like tiling in the bathroom, kitchen or paved areas.

2 Tessellations in the classroom

Talk about any tessellations that the children can see in the classroom or school, such as floor tiles, ceiling tiles, wired glass in doors, etc. Look for tessellations of one shape such as the square or the rectangle.

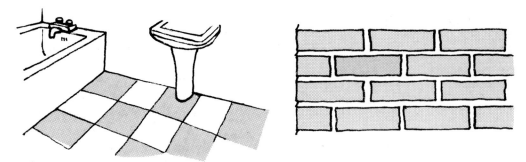

Look for any examples where a number of different shapes are tessellating and making repeating patterns. For example, paved areas are often made up of rectangles and squares.

3 Shapes that don't tessellate

Ask the children to look for shapes that don't tessellate. For example, look at a collection of tins or paint pots pushed together to see that circles or cylinders don't tessellate. Ask the children why they don't tessellate.

Ask the children to tell you where they have seen plane (two-dimensional) shapes tessellating and solid (three-dimensional) shapes tessellating.

LINKS WITH THE ENVIRONMENT

- Look for tessellations as children come to school. These might include paving stones, zebra crossings, shopping precinct floors.
- Some firm's logos show tessellations.
- Some boxes in supermarkets tessellate.
- Brick walls have tessellating patterns.
- Windows can show tessellations. What other parts of buildings show tessellations – tiles around swimming baths, mosaic pictures etc.?

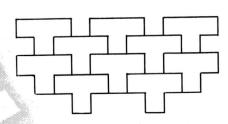

NOTES ON INVESTIGATIONS

Section A

Do the children appreciate that there should be a basic pattern that repeats rather than a haphazard arrangement?
    Do they relate the pattern to the environment?
    Do they draw the obvious basic patterns first? For example,

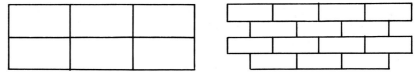

Do they try more complicated tessellations such as parquet floors?

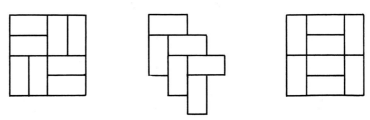

Section B

Do the children investigate more than one possibility? Are they careful to match the sides of the equilateral triangles? Are they curious about the names of the shapes they have made?
    Do they count the number of sides of other shapes they make?

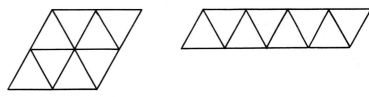

Section C

Provide some templates whose sides are matched in length.
    Do the children explore these templates or shapes and realise that if the sides match in length they are likely to give the best tessellations? Do they adopt a system to produce a tessellating pattern?
    Three possible solutions:

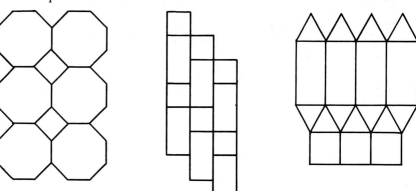

Number 8

Purpose

- To introduce multiplication by 7 and 8
- To revise multiplication of two digits by one digit
- To revise multiplication by 10

Materials

Squared paper

Vocabulary

Days, weeks, answers, tables, multiply, difference, missing number, pattern, odd, table, easiest way, follow

TEACHING POINTS

1 Sets of 8

Ask the children to think of sets of 8. For example, spiders' legs (in pupils' book), octopus, fingers (without thumbs), octaves on a piano, rowing eights.

2 Building eights

Use rows of 8 children to build the table as far as your class numbers allow.

$1 \times 8 = 8$

$2 \times 8 = 16$

$3 \times 8 = 24$

$4 \times 8 = 32$

Two chairs have 8 legs between them. Make rows of pairs of chairs. Invent a land where inhabitants have 8 legs or eyes or arms. Ask the children to draw the socks or gloves for 6 of the octopeople. How many wellingtons would 3 of them have? This can produce some fun display work.

3 The table of eights

Build up the table of eights on squared paper.

1	2	3	4	5	6	7	8
9	10	11	12	13	14	15	16
17	18	19	20	21	22	23	24
25	26	27	28	29	30	31	32
33	34	35	36	37	38	39	40
41	42	43	44	45	46	47	48
49	50	51	52	53	54	55	56
57	58	59	60	61	62	63	64
65	66	67	68	69	70	71	72
73	74	75	76	77	78	79	80

Talk about the pattern of the numbers:

- They are all even.
- The last digit repeats: 8   16   24   32   40   48   56   64   72   80

4 Patterns of 7

Ask the children to think of sevens. The days in a week is the most obvious one here. Look at calendars and diaries. Ask how many days there are in 2 weeks, 10 weeks, etc.

Use the calendars to find out how many days in the school holidays – Christmas, Easter, summer, half-terms.

5 The table of sevens

Make a class chart for seven days based on daily events or weather. For example,

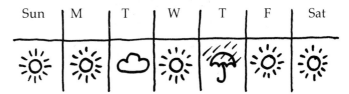

Write the table of sevens.

6 Table square

Combine all the tables so far and build a multiplication square. Show the children how to use it.

The children can be given a partially completed square to complete. They can also time how long it takes to complete a square, and try to do it faster each day.

x	1	2	3	4	5	6	7	8
1	1	2	3	4	5	6	7	8
2	2	4	6	8	10	12	14	16
3	3	6	9	12	15	18	21	24
4	4	8	12	16	20	24	28	32
5	5	10	15	20	25	30	35	40
6	6	12	18	24	30	36	42	48
7	7	14	21	28	35	42	49	56
8	8	16	24	32	40	48	56	64

7 Patterns of tens

Talk about patterns of tens. Write the numbers 10, 20, 30, 40, 50, 60, 70, 80, 90, 100. Can they see a pattern where all the numbers end in 0?

Make displays of pairs of gloves or hand prints (not feet as these are in the pupils' book).

8 Multiplication of two digits by one digit

Show the children how to record these and to work them out. Use your own words and method, and see if the children have developed any methods of their own.

```
    T U
    2 4
×     8
    ───
```

9 Link with addition

Do the children realise that addition and multiplication are related?

$$8 + 8 + 8 = 3 \times 8$$

10 Function machines

Talk with the children about simple function machines. The design can take many forms, for example,

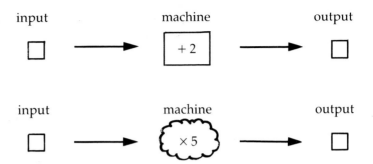

Ask the children to describe what this machine is doing to the left-hand numbers (input) to get to the right-hand numbers (output). What is the function?

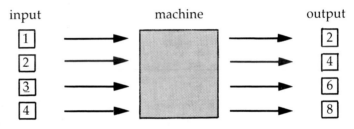

Use machines to multiply numbers by 7, by 8 and by 10.

Ask the children to find the input numbers in the machine if the output numbers are 30, 50, 60, 80, 90.

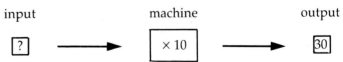

The machine can be made more difficult according the the ability of the children as shown in this example.

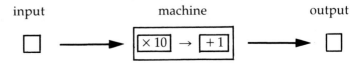

Make a machine

Copy and then duplicate some function machines. Let the children make up their own input and function and then find the output.

11 Mental work

Practise counting in 7, 8 and 10 forward and backward.

Multiply numbers by 10. For example, 3×10. Do they look for the pattern and use this when multiplying other numbers by 10? For example, $3 \times 10 = \underline{3}0$, $12 \times 10 = \underline{12}0$

Practise tables in a variety of ways. Draw a table clock and point to different numbers for the children to multiply by the central number.

Find missing tables: $7 \times \square = 56$ or $8 \times \square = 32$.

Solve word problems using multiplication.

Ask questions which link addition and multiplication. For example, write $3 + 3 + 3 + 3 + 3 + 3$ as a multiplication sentence, 6×3.

Look for easy ways of multiplying numbers such as $2 \times 5 \times 8$ and $6 \times 5 \times 2$, for example by multiplying 2×5 first.

12 Games to play

NUMBER BONDS

Choose a number on the table square such as 40. Ask the children to give multiplication bonds to make that number. For example, 5×8 or 4×10. One point is scored for each correct number bond.

SHUFFLE

Make a set of cards for the table of 7. Shuffle and give them out, one to each child. Can the children holding them come and stand in order? Can they stand in reverse order? Which group can do this the fastest? If you remove one card before dealing them out, can they discover which one is missing?

GIVE US A CLUE

Let someone choose a number such as 35. The other children have to guess which one it is from clues, like 'the 5th one in the table of sevens' or 'between 28 and 42'.

BUZZ

The class takes turns in counting in ones. They must say 'Buzz' when they come to a multiple of 8. For example, 1, 2, 3, 4, 5, 6, 7, Buzz, 9, 10, . . .

RACES

Have a set of numbers in the table of 8 (i.e. 8, 16, 24, 32, 40, 48, 56, 64, 72, 80) spread out (perhaps on the hall floor). Arrange the children in teams. Call out 5×8. One child from each team has to try to find the answer from the floor cards. The first one to pick it up scores one point for their team.

USING THE CALCULATOR   Use the constant function to reinforce the tables of 10, 8 and 7.
    Use the calculator to extend the work on days of the week. For example,

- How many days are in 10 weeks?
- How many days in 52 weeks?
- How many extra days are there in a normal year?
- How many extra days in a leap year?

A game to play

NEAREST TO 100

Two children use one calculator. The first player enters any number between 1 and 10. The second player tries to reach 100 or get as near to it as possible by multiplying with different numbers. For example, suppose the first player enters 2. The second player multiplies by 5 and then by 10. i.e. $2 \times 5 = 10$, $10 \times 10 = 100$. The players then change over. Two points are awarded for reaching 100 exactly. If no-one scores 100 exactly, one point is awarded for the nearest score to 100. The winner is the first to reach 10 points.

LINKS WITH THE ENVIRONMENT

Talk about everyday situations involving 7, 8 and 10.

- Nature – spiders and octopi with 8 legs
- One kind of ladybird has 7 black spots
- Have the children read *Charlotte's Web* by E.B. White?
- Sport – 7 players in a netball team, 8 running lanes in athletics, rowing eights, 8 lanes in the swimming baths
- Music – notes in an octave. Tonic sol-fa – 'Do-re-me' song from 'The Sound of Music'
- Diaries and calendars – look at all the different types. Talk about famous ones, for example, Samuel Pepys, Anne Frank, and an Edwardian Lady
- Poetry – poems about days of birth, for example, 'Monday's child is fair of face' and 'Monday's child is fairly tough'. Both these poems are in *Clever Polly and the Stupid Wolf*, by Catherine Storr, in the chapter entitled 'Monday's Child'
- Travel – look in travel brochures at the length of holidays in weeks and days. How many weeks and days did it take famous sailors like Francis Chichester to sail round the world?
- Crayons and felt tips often come in packets of 8.
- Are any bus numbers in the 7, 8 or 10 multiplication tables?

NOTES ON INVESTIGATIONS

Section A

Are the children aware of the pattern when multiplying by 10? Do they try it for other number patterns of their own? Do they come to realise that the new pattern will always end in 0?

Section B

Do the children find that the difference is 2 each time? Are they systematic in trying four numbers that follow each other? For example,   1, 2, 3, 4;   2, 3, 4, 5;   3, 4, 5, 6.
Do any of the children try it with larger numbers and use a calculator?

Section C

Do the children find difficulty in completing the missing numbers initially? Do they choose single-digit numbers for the input numbers?
Do they appreciate that an odd number ends in 1, 3, 5, 7 and 9?
When multiplying by 8, do they realise that they must add any odd number to make the output odd?

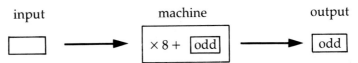

When multiplying by 7, do they realise that when an even number is the input an odd number must be added, and vice versa?

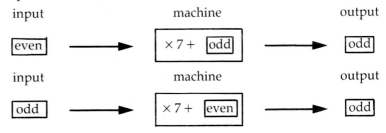

Purpose

- To introduce cm^2 as a standard unit for measuring area

Materials

1 cm squared paper, string, crayons, tracing paper, transparent grid

Vocabulary

Square centimetre, squares, area, different shapes, half, rectangle, total, greatest

TEACHING POINTS   **1 Revise area**

Remind the children that area is the amount of surface covered by a shape, and that we measure area by counting squares.

Draw a block shape on the board. Ask the children to state its area. For example,

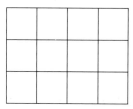

Area = ☐ squares

2 Revise the half square method

Talk with the children about finding the approximate area of irregular shapes.

- Count all the whole squares first.
- Count half squares, or greater, as whole squares.
- Don't count anything less than half a square.

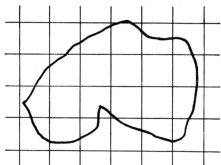

Area = ☐ squares

Some children may find it helpful to mark with a dot or colour in the squares they have counted.

Show the children how to record the area of a shape.

3 The square centimetre (cm²) as the standard unit

Talk with the children about the problems of describing area if different sizes of squares are used to record an area of, say, 15 squares. Explain that we use a standard unit to count area. This is the square centimetre (cm²).

Show them how to write square centimetres as cm².

4 Finding area using cm ^{2}

Ask the children to draw a number of shapes on 1 cm squared paper and to record each area in cm^2.

Ask them to draw a picture or pattern using a fixed area, for example, 20 cm^2. These can be cut out to make a display which could lead to an interesting discussion on the conservation of area.

A game to play

THREE SQUARES

This is a game for two players. Give the children a 10 cm × 10 cm grid, and a different coloured crayon each. The players take turns to colour an area of 3 cm^2. The squares must be edge matched. For example

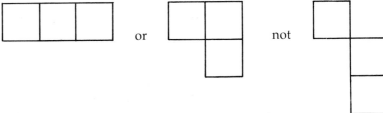

The winner is the player who covers the most 3 cm^2 areas.

5 Using a grid sheet

Show the children how to use a centimetre square transparent grid sheet or one marked on tracing paper. This can be used to place over shapes or objects like leaves in order to count their area.

LINKS WITH THE ENVIRONMENT

- Talk with the children about where we might see areas in square centimetres – graph paper, mosaic pictures and patterns.
- The area of children's body parts – for example, hands or feet – could be investigated and displayed.
- The area of book covers or pages – how much of the page area does a picture cover?

NOTES ON INVESTIGATIONS

Section A

Do the children make a pleasing design for the patchwork? Do they use 24 squares for their rectangle? Do they use some half squares? Do the same colours on both designs have the same area?

Section B

Do the children use a variety of colours? Do they use the half square method to measure the area? Do they use the correct notation to record the area of each colour?

Section C

Do the children realise that it is possible to make many different areas using the string? Do they realise that the closer you get to a circle the larger the area?

Number 9

Purpose

- To introduce division of tens and units by 7 and 8
- To introduce division with remainders

Materials

Structural apparatus, pack of children's playing cards, counters

Vocabulary

Charts, groups, remainder, share between, divide exactly, division, dividing, smaller than, answer

TEACHING POINTS   **1 Tables of 7 and 8**

Revise the tables of 7 and 8 with the children by counting on in 7 or 8. Can they put the multiples of 7 in order using number cards?

Try the same for the multiples of 8.

2 Multiplication square

Remind the children about the multiplication square and how to use it to multiply numbers. Let them practise this.

Show them how to use the multiplication square for division.

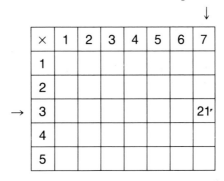

$$3 \times 7 = 21$$
$$21 \div 7 = 3$$

Talk about the link between multiplication and division. For example, using 4, 8 and 32, the following number bonds can be written

$$4 \times 8 = 32 \qquad 32 \div 8 = 4$$
$$8 \times 4 = 32 \qquad 32 \div 4 = 8$$

Let the children practise this.

A game to play

FIND THE DIVISION

This can be played in pairs or teams. One child asks a second to answer a division question using the multiplication square. One point is scored for every correct answer. The asker writes the answer down first and uses it to check the reply.

The winner is the player (or team) with the highest score after an agreed number of questions.

3 Remainders

Use a group of children to show that things do not always divide equally. For example, ask 11 children to form groups of three. Ask, 'Are there any left over?'

Talk about the remainder and how to record it (usually r or rem).

$$\begin{array}{r} 3\,r\,2 \\ 3\overline{)11} \end{array}$$

Give plenty of practice with this.

Games to play

ISLANDS

This game needs plenty of space.

Spread out some small mats to act as islands. The children sit scattered around amongst the islands.

When a number is called out, they get into groups of that number and sit on an island. Any children not in a group are the remainder.

PIRATES

Plenty of space is needed for this game.

Choose a few children to be pirates. The others need team bands tucked in loosely like tails.

When a number is called out, the pirates chase after the bands and make up groups of that number. When their bands are taken, children sit down.

When all bands have been taken, the 'pirates' see how many groups they have made, and how many bands are the remainder.

COLLECT A CUBE

Divide the children into teams. Each child must be given the same number of cubes. When a number is called out, the teams have to put their cubes into groups of that number.

The first team to finish sends one child to write the division on a piece of paper or the board. If it is correct, that team gains a point.

The winning team is the one with the most points after a specified length of time.

4 Division with 'exchanging'

Use structural apparatus to explain that we first divide the tens into equal groups.

$$3 \overline{)\, 42} \quad \rightarrow \quad 3 \overline{)\, 4^12}^{\,1\ 4}$$

Any extra tens are changed into units, added to the units already there and then shared into equal groups.

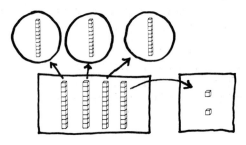 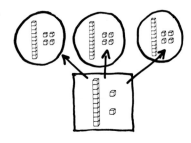

Include remainders and show the children how to record them:

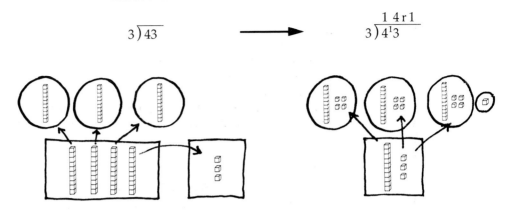

Games to play

MULTIVIDE

Call out a number such as 16. Ask the children to write out a multiplication and a division sentence for it, using a multiplication square if necessary. For example,

$$4 \times 4 = 16 \qquad 16 \div 2 = 8$$

PAIRS

Lay out some cards for children to put into pairs. Time them to see how quickly they can be put into pairs. Let another group try to beat the record.

$$\boxed{16 \div 8 = 2} \qquad \boxed{8 \times 2 = 16}$$

FIND THE MOST

How many number sentences can the children find for a given number such as 12? Who can find the most in a given time?

CHANGE THE SIGN

One child calls out a multiplication sentence and another has to call it out as a division sentence. For example,

> five sevens are thirty-five
> there are seven fives in thirty-five
> there are five sevens in thirty-five
> thirty-five divided by five is seven, etc.

5 Mental work

Ask children simple division bonds such as $12 \div 3$, $28 \div 7$. Use different words to ask the questions such as, 'How many 3s in 15?' 'Share 15 by 3,' 'What do we divide 15 by to give an answer of 3?' or ask the children verbal division problems like 'John shared 16 cards between 4 children. How many did each get?'

Use some questions that involve remainders and give the children practice in rounding answers up or down.

If an egg box holds 6 eggs, how many boxes are needed to hold 20 eggs?

We need 4 boxes. 3 boxes will be full and the other box will have only 2 eggs.

How many boxes can be completely filled?

3 boxes are completely full and there aren't enough left to fill one more.

USING THE CALCULATOR   Remind the children how to divide using the calculator. Talk about what happens if the number does not divide exactly, i.e. there are numbers after the point.

A game to play

Ask the first child to enter a division where there is no remainder, like $28 \div 7$, when the answer will be a whole number. One point is scored for a whole number. If the answer does not give a whole number a point goes to the opponent.

The game can be played in various ways. For example, the first number must be two digits or the number must be divided by 7, 8 etc.

The game may be played in reverse so that the child has to enter a division where the answer is not a whole number.

LINKS WITH THE ENVIRONMENT   Talk with the children about division situations in everyday life.

- Team or group games when the teams or groups do not work out exactly. What happens to the extras?
- Sharing things in school
- Arranging books on shelves
- Baking – arranging cakes on trays, etc.

- Arranging equal numbers of bulbs in bowls
- Dealing out cards in a game
- Allocating places in cars to attend sports fixtures
- Sitting at tables in the dining hall

NOTES ON INVESTIGATIONS

Section A

Do the children relate this division problem to multiplication? Do any make use of the charts in the pupils' book?

One method would be to write down the multiples of 7 and see which could be made using two of cards:

7	14	21	28	35	42	49	56	63	70
only	no	no							no
one	card	card							zero
card	1	1							card

Similarly for 8

8	16	24	32	40	48	56	64	72	80
only	no			no					no
one	card			zero					zero
card	1			card					card

Section B

Do the children develop any system? Here are some ideas. Find one number that works and then add 7 for the next number, etc.
Or write out multiples of 7 and add 2 to each.
Or start with a number and count on in sevens, such as 2, 9, 16, . . .

Section C

Do the children realise that this can be solved easily by using multiplication? For example, starting at 1:

$$1 \times 2 \times 3 \times 5 = 30 \quad \text{gives} \quad 30 \div 2 \div 3 \div 5 = 1$$

Do any children divide by the same number each time?

$$8 \div 2 \div 2 \div 2 = 1$$

Do any children divide numbers by 1?

Data 2

Purpose

- To introduce co-ordinates in the first quadrant
- To introduce the notation (2, 3) for finding position

Materials

Squared paper

Vocabulary

Co-ordinates, join, points, grid, order, plan, outer, pattern, top, bottom, small

TEACHING POINTS

1 Grids and points

Talk about how to find positions on grids. Explain that positions can be marked by points, and the points are where the lines cross or intersect.

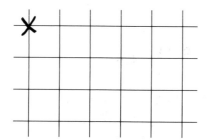

2 Notation

Talk about how we can plot the positions of these points. Show the children how the grids have numbers along the bottom (horizontal axis) and up the side (vertical axis).

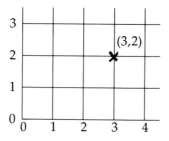

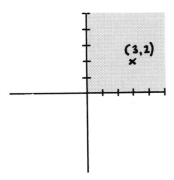

Show the children how to read the number along the bottom first and then the number up the side. For example, the point shown on the grid is at (3, 2).

NB. The National Curriculum states that at first, co-ordinates should be in the first quadrant with both axes showing positive numbers. In later National Curriculum levels all four quadrants are used, thereby involving negative numbers.

3 Joining co-ordinates

Show the children how they can join co-ordinates to draw pictures or letters. For example, they can draw the Z on squared paper using (1, 3) → (3, 3) → (1, 1) → (3, 1).

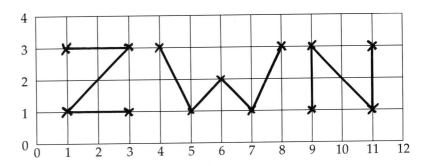

Can they give the co-ordinates for these letters?

W (4, 3) → (   ) → (   ) → (   ) → (   )
N (9, 1) → (   ) → (   ) → (   )

Ask some children to write the co-ordinates of a letter and ask the others to draw it.

Write the co-ordinates of a house and ask the children to draw it on squared paper. Ask them to draw and write their own co-ordinates for a door and two windows.

Ask the children to draw their own picture and co-ordinates.

4 Games to play

INITIALS

Ask the children to mark two sets of axes on squared paper.

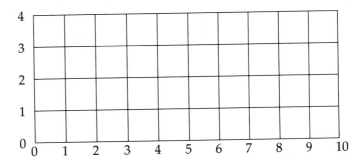

Ask them to draw their initials on one of their grids in block letters using a ruler. For example,

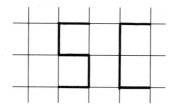

Ask them to write the co-ordinates for these letters on another piece of paper. The 'co-ordinate' papers are then shuffled and distributed round the class. The children have to find out whose piece of paper they have by using the co-ordinates to draw the initials on the other grid.

PLAYGROUND CO-ORDINATES

Mark a grid on the playground or hall floor and number it. Make a small card for each pair of co-ordinates, and put the cards in a box.

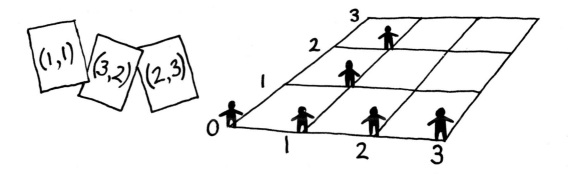

At a given signal the children run to a different co-ordinate each. Ask a child to pick a card out of the box. Whoever is standing on the co-ordinate chosen is out. The card is put back in the box. Continue the game until one child (the winner) is left.

A variation is to award the child on the chosen co-ordinate 1 point. The winner is the first child to score 5 points.

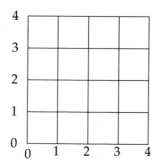

CO-ORDINATE QUIZ GAME

Draw a grid on a large piece of paper or board. Make up a mathematical or general knowledge question for each pair of co-ordinates.

Put the children into two teams and give each team a colour. Each player in a team in turn selects a pair of co-ordinates and is asked the matching question.

When the correct answer is given a star is put on that point. The winning team is the first to make a line of five stars.

LINKS WITH THE ENVIRONMENT

Talk with the children about using co-ordinates in everyday life. For example:

- Find places on maps and plans.
- Make a simple map of an imaginary village, countryside, harbour or castle and show particular features using co-ordinates.
- Artwork. Plan designs and give co-ordinates. Link these to history, for example, shields, designs of buildings, etc.
- Look for co-ordinates on Ordnance Survey maps of the local area. This can be interesting and relevant particularly when going on school trips.

NOTES ON INVESTIGATIONS

Section A

A picture or discussion on the shape of old keys is probably necessary here.

Do the children write the co-ordinates correctly? Are the co-ordinates in the correct order? Do they complete the picture when joined?

Section B

Do the children draw some more shields the same size and then design a pattern (coat of arms) on them to colour? Do they write the co-ordinates correctly, and join them with straight lines?

Section C

Do the children use reference books and find interesting features for their castles? Do they appreciate that the features chosen must be static ones, such as windows, to be shown on the grid? Do they plan the towers, buildings and gate with co-ordinates in mind? Do they use a sufficiently large grid? Do they write the co-ordinates correctly?

Money 2

Purpose

- To multiply pence with 'carrying' to make £ and p
- To link addition and multiplication of money
- To revise writing pence as pounds

Materials

Coins

Vocabulary

Pounds, pence, cost, change, sets of coins, money, altogether, total cost, chart, calculator

TEACHING POINTS

1 Writing in pounds

Talk with the children about how to write pence as pounds, using the £ sign. For example,   50p = £0.50   327p = £3.27. Ask the children to write all the coin values in this way.

2 Cost of more than one

Talk about the times when we buy more than one thing:

- bus or train fares
- sweets or crisps
- stamps
- tins of dog or cat food
- tickets to the theatre, cinema, football match or school play
- a set of calculators for the class

Talk about a local bus ride for a number of children in the class. How much is a child's fare?

If nine children go and pay 13p each, how do we work it out? It could be written like this:

$$13p + 13p + 13p + 13p + 13p + 13p + 13p + 13p + 13p$$

Ask if they can see a shorter way of writing it. For example,

$$9 \times 13p$$

Talk about ways of recording this. For example,

$$
\begin{array}{ccc}
£ & \text{or} & p \\
0.13 & & 13 \\
\times \quad 9 & & \times \quad 9 \\
\hline
1.17 & & 117 = £1.17 \\
\end{array}
$$

cup of tea
20p

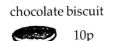

chocolate biscuit
10p

3 Games to play

CAFÉ

Sit the children in groups of 2, 3, 4 or 5. Make cards showing realistic prices.

Let each group choose two cards and work out the total cost of this snack for the group. The cards and the correct plastic money is brought out for the teacher to check.

BINGO

Make out bingo cards for children with amounts of money written in £.

£0.50	£0.20	£0.45
£0.70	£0.75	£1.20

Call out all the different amounts, such as 50p; the child who has this amount on their card covers it with a counter. The winner is the first child to cover their card.

A variation of this might be the first to cover a line. If a larger card is used then the winner can be the first to cover a line, diagonally, horizontally or vertically.

4 How many can you buy?

Talk about costs of sweets and comics and how many of each can be bought with a given amount of money, for example, pocket money.

Questions can also be related to the school play in the pupils' book. For example, suppose three children have £1.50 to spend between them. Talk about the different ways they can spend the money such as all going to the school play on a Thursday night ($3 \times 25p = 75p$), buying a programme each ($3 \times 6p = 18p$) and an orange drink each ($3 \times 11p = 33p$). Total cost £1.26. What other possibilities are there? How much money, if any, will they have left over?

USING THE CALCULATOR

Games to play

CALL OUT

You need two teams of children. One child from each team has a calculator.

Call out '35p'. The first team to show 0.35 on their calculator scores a point.

CHECK OUT

Put out two piles of cards, one set showing numbers, the other set showing prices in pence. Each team turns over a top card in each pile:

The calculator is used to find the answer. A correct answer scores a point for the team, but answers must be found on the first attempt in order to score.

LINKS WITH THE ENVIRONMENT

- Talk about buying tickets for theatre, cinema, travel, etc.
  Set up a booking office for a class play.
  Sell tickets and programmes using plastic money.
- Eating out. Make up a menu. Plan a meal and its cost. Pretend to order a take-away meal by phone and work out the bill on a calculator.
- Sports occasions. Work out the cost of tickets for a family or class.

NOTES ON INVESTIGATIONS

Section A

Do the children devise a system for finding coins of the same value? Do they, for example, work through the coins in order of value?

$$30 \times 1p \qquad 15 \times 2p \qquad 6 \times 5p \qquad 3 \times 10p$$

Section B

Do the children consider ways of showing the information? For example, do they use a table?

1	2	3	4	5	6
12p	24p	36p	48p	60p	72p

Do they use a calculator to help? Do they recognise the pattern of adding 12p each time?

Section C

Children will not have attempted this calculation before. Do they find a way to resolve it without a calculator? For example, do they add up 18p twenty-five times? Or do they work out $(25 \times 10p) + (25 \times 8p)$? Can they explain what they have done?

Purpose

- To introduce thirds of shapes, numbers and objects.

Materials

Squared paper, clock stamp

Vocabulary

One third, two thirds, fraction, half, shapes, whole shape, different, thousands, middle, first, last, small, dividing, circular, empty, number, tableaux, clock faces

TEACHING POINTS

1 Thirds

Talk about thirds. Explain or show that a cake or chocolate bar may be cut or broken into three equal pieces. Each part is one third.

Talk about how to write $\frac{1}{3}$ and what it means: 1 out of 3 equal parts.

2 Thirds of shapes

Ask the children to fold a paper rectangle into three equal pieces. This can be done by careful folding or by measuring with a ruler first. Label each part $\frac{1}{3}$.

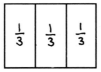

Mark '1' or '1 whole' on the other side and talk about the equivalence. Hang this up as a mobile.

 turn over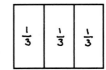

3 Fraction wall

Give the children two equal rectangular strips of paper. Ask them to mark '1' or '1 whole' on the first strip and stick it in their books.

Ask them to check that the second strip is the same length as the first, and then to fold (or measure) it into 3 equal parts. Give them helpful instructions in order to ensure accuracy.
'Check that they are equal by matching the three parts.'
'Each part is one third of the whole. Don't forget to label them.'

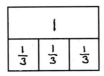

Ask 'How many thirds make the whole?'
Explain that we write 'two thirds' as $\frac{2}{3}$ (and not $2\frac{1}{3}$).
Ask the children to write the fractions in words as well as symbols.

4 Thirds of numbers

Draw a number of circles, say 3, on paper or on the board. Ask a child to colour $\frac{1}{3}$ of the circles, and then
'How many of the circles are not coloured?'
'What fraction is this?'
 Ask the children to draw six equal shapes and colour $\frac{1}{3}$ of them.

 Ask the children to draw six squares joined together. For example,

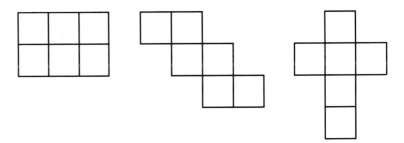

Ask them to colour $\frac{1}{3}$ red and $\frac{2}{3}$ green in different ways.

'How many squares are red?'
'What fraction is red?'
'How many squares are green?'
'What fraction is green?'
'What is $\frac{1}{3}$ of six squares?'
'What is $\frac{2}{3}$ of six squares?'

5 A game to play

BRING ME A FRACTION

Play the game in two teams or groups. Give each team six counters. Ask a player from each team to bring you a fraction (e.g. $\frac{1}{3}$ or $\frac{2}{3}$) of the counters. The first player to bring the correct number of counters scores one point for their team.

The game could be extended by using a larger number of counters.

6 Completing shapes

Talk with the children about drawing a whole picture when only given a part. For example,

$\boxed{\frac{1}{3}}$ or $\triangle\frac{1}{3}$ or $\overset{\text{O}}{,}\overset{\text{O}}{\underset{3}{\frac{1}{3}}}$

Ask the children to draw the whole picture.

7 Mental Work

After practice on the activities in 1–6 ask the children to work out answers to problems like these.

- $\frac{1}{3}$ of 3, 6, 9, 12, 15, 18, 21, 24
- $\frac{2}{3}$ of 3, 6, 9, 12 (for those able to cope with this)
- Simple word problems involving thirds.

A game to play

You need a board for each player, counters and a die.

1 whole	$\frac{1}{3}$
$\frac{2}{3}$	one third

Players take turns to throw the die and pick up that number of counters. When a player has enough counters, these are placed on the correct section of the board to show the fraction. The winner is the first to complete the board.

USING THE CALCULATOR Show the children how to find $\frac{1}{3}$ of numbers using the calculator. For example, to find $\frac{1}{3}$ of 6 we divide 6 by 3. Enter $\boxed{6}\,\boxed{\div}\,\boxed{3}\,\boxed{=}$

The numbers must be multiples of 3 in order to avoid decimals when dividing.

LINKS WITH THE ENVIRONMENT

Talk about everyday situations involving thirds.

- We might share cake, chocolate, sweets, rock or money into three equal parts.
- Some flags are divided into thirds.
- We might use $\frac{1}{3}$ pint of milk when baking.
- Some organisations use logos involving three equal sections. For example, the Aer Lingus symbol and the three legs symbol from the Isle of Man.

NOTES ON INVESTIGATIONS

Section A

Do the children divide the 18 squares into thirds?

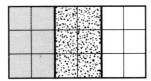 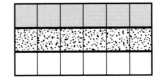

Do they find several different ways to do it? In finding the other ways, do they first work out that $\frac{1}{3}$ of 18 is 6?

Section B

Do the children choose a number of bulbs which will divide exactly into thirds? Do they use the pattern 3, 6, 9, 12, 15, 18, 21, . . . ? Do they divide by 3 to find $\frac{1}{3}$ and double their answer to find $\frac{2}{3}$? Do they find $\frac{1}{3}$ and realise that the number of bulbs left must be $\frac{2}{3}$?

Section C

Do the children adopt a system for dividing the clock faces into thirds? For example,

12–4–8

1–5–9

2–6–10

Length 2

Purpose

- To find perimeters of shapes

Materials

Rulers, equilateral triangles, squared paper

Vocabulary

Perimeter, distance, largest, smallest, difference, square, length, hexagon, equilateral triangle, rectangle, ruler, centimetre, plane shapes, sides

TEACHING POINTS

1 Introducing perimeter

Talk with the children about the boundary of a cricket pitch or a soccer pitch. Why do we need boundaries? Introduce the term 'perimeter' as the distance round the edge (or boundary) of a shape. Ask what we mean by the perimeter of the classroom. How could we find it?

2 Measuring perimeter

Talk about how to measure the perimeter of the classroom and the best unit to use for this.

Draw or find some shapes in the school yard or playground. Ask the children to walk round the perimeter. This could be measured by using tapes or trundle wheels and the perimeter found to the nearest metre.

Let the children measure the perimeters of smaller things such as books, crayon boxes, etc. using their rulers. Measure to the nearest centimetre. Talk about which is the best unit to use in each case, centimetres or metres, and why.

Measure the perimeters of some plane shapes such as triangles or squares.

The perimeter
is 14 cm

3 Drawing shapes

Draw some shapes on the board and write their measurements. Ask the children to work out the perimeters.

Ask the children to draw some shapes on squared paper and find the perimeter.

Give the children a measurement, such as 18 cm, and ask them to draw a shape with this perimeter using squared paper.

A game to play

HOW MANY PERIMETERS?

Put the children into groups. Give each group a sheet of squared paper. Call out a perimeter measurement, such as 20 cm. Which group can draw the most shapes, each with a perimeter of 20 cm?

4 Investigating squares

Let the children draw a 1 cm square on squared paper and find its perimeter (4 cm). Ask them to draw another square, adding 1 cm to each side. What happens to the perimeter? Add another 1 cm to each side, and find the perimeter. Do the children see the pattern of the perimeter increasing by 4 cm each time?

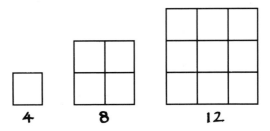

5 Investigating rectangles

Let the children draw a rectangle on squared paper and find its perimeter. Ask them to add 1 cm to each side. What happens to the perimeter? Add another 1 cm to each side. Do they see the pattern of the perimeter increasing by 4 cm each time?

6 Regular shapes

Ask the children to draw round some templates of regular shapes and to find the perimeters. Talk about how this might be done for shapes such as the pentagon – either add up the five sides or measure one side and multiply it by five. This gives a good link between addition and multiplication.

7 Feet

Children might be interested in finding the perimeter of their foot by drawing round it and measuring the perimeter using string.

8 Mental work

Can the children think of quick ways of finding perimeters?

- Quick addition. Look for easy number bonds first:

  (4 cm + 6 cm) + (4 cm + 6 cm)
      10 cm + 10 cm

- Links between addition and multiplication:

  10 cm + 10 cm + 10 cm + 10 cm = 4 × 10 cm

- Doubling numbers:

  4 cm + 6 cm + 4 cm + 6 cm
  (2 × 4 cm) + (2 × 6 cm)

9 Another investigation

Draw a 4 × 4 square and find the perimeter. Find the perimeter of
a quarter of it, half of it, three quarters of it:
Talk about the different answers children find.

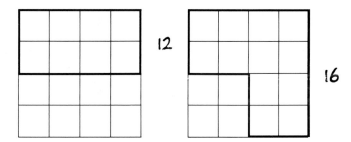

**USING THE
CALCULATOR**
Give the children some calculator problems. For example, a Giant
Tortoise walks 4 metres in 1 minute. How long will it take to walk
around the playground perimeter? (A trundle wheel may be needed to
find the perimeters.)

**LINKS WITH THE
ENVIRONMENT**

- Buying fencing for home or the school garden. How much is
  needed?
- Sports fields and pitches and their perimeters.
- Discuss why high-rise tower blocks are often built in confined
  spaces (many homes in a limited perimeter).
- Art. Making frames and borders for pictures.
- Jig-saws. What does 24 cm × 30 cm mean? Will it fit on a table?
- Planning furniture for rooms, for example, fitting a bed or
  cupboard into an alcove.

NOTES ON INVESTIGATIONS

Section A

Do the children work logically? Do they appreciate that, for rectangles, adjacent sides must add up to 12 cm and that there are a variety of answers?

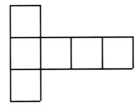

Do they attempt shapes other than rectangles?

Section B

Many of the shapes made using six squares (hexominoes) have a perimeter of 14 cm when drawn on 1 cm squared paper. For example,

This could be extended to finding the hexomino with the smallest perimeter.

Section C

Do the children try to show as many edges as possible to get the largest perimeter? For example,

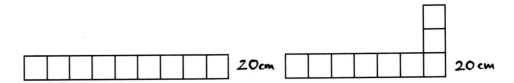

Do they try to 'lose' as many edges as possible to get the smallest perimeter?

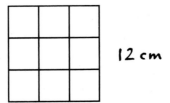

Do the children find perimeters between 12 cm and 20 cm?

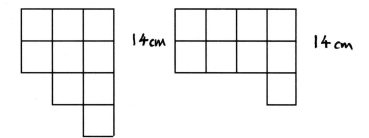

Purpose

- To multiply and divide using grams

Materials

Balance scales, soft toys, weights, selection of spare clothes

Vocabulary

Estimate, different, most, least, weights, grams, altogether, heavier

TEACHING POINTS

1 Estimating and weighing in grams

Ask the children to look at the weights for the balance scales. Let them hold a weight, for example 100 g, and ask them to find something that they think is about that weight. Let them check their estimates by weighing.

2 Matching weights

Give a group of children four different weights and four objects of the same approximate weights. For example, 50 g, 100 g, 200 g, 500 g. Ask the children to match an object to a weight without weighing it and then to check by weighing and to consider whether their estimates were sensible.

3 Multiplication/repeated addition

Ask a child to weigh a small object such as a chocolate biscuit (20 g). If they had four of these, how much would they weigh altogether?

$$20\,g + 20\,g + 20\,g + 20\,g = 80g$$

Ask if the children can think of another way to record it. For example,

$$
\begin{array}{r}
g \\
20 \\
\times\ \underline{4} \\
\overline{}
\end{array}
$$

Explain that the multiplication of weight in grams can be set down and multiplied in the same way as tens and units.

4 Division/repeated subtraction

Set the children a problem like this.
'A bag of biscuits weighs 80 g. Each biscuit weights 8 g. How many biscuits are in the bag?'
Can this be solved by subtraction?

$$80\,g - 8\,g - 8\,g - 8\,g - 8\,g - 8\,g - 8\,g - 8\,g - 8\,g - 8\,g - 8\,g = 0$$

Can the children suggest another way to work it out?

$$
\begin{array}{r}
g\ \ \ \ \\
\overline{} \\
8\,)\,\overline{80}
\end{array}
$$

Give the children practice in dividing like this. Remind them that dividing weights in grams is done in the same way as dividing numbers.

5 Weighing activities

Let the children weigh some small objects in the classroom. Ask them to weigh one and then work out the weight of 2, 3, 4, etc. Ask them whether their answers are sensible ones.

The children can also weigh several identical objects (carefully chosen by the teacher for division without remainders!). Ask them to work out the weight of one and then check with the balance scales.

6 Games to play

GUESS THE ORDER

This can be played in teams. Give the team of children four things, all weighing less than 100 g. Ask them to put the objects in order of weight by estimating and write the answer down. Then check the objects on the scales. If the order was correct, the team scores a point.

FIND THE ANSWER

Make flash cards with divisions on one side and the answer on the
back, for example,

| 50 g ÷ 5 | | 10 g |

Make another set of answer cards.

   Divide the class into two teams. A child from one team holds up a
division flash card. A child from the other team chooses a card from
the answer pack and holds that up. The first child checks if the answer
corresponds to that on the back of the card. If it does, the child who
gave the answer scores a point for the team.

WEIGHT RACE

Put, for example, 15 g + 15 g + 15 g + 15 g on the board. Ask two
children to work out the answer, one by addition, the other by
multiplication. Who does it first?

7 Further weighing and estimating

As an interesting class activity linked to the pupils' pages, let the
children weigh one or two of their own scarves, jumpers, gloves, etc.
If they are made of more than one colour of wool, let the children try to
estimate the approximate weight of each colour. Ask them whether
their answers are sensible.

   This is obviously quite difficult and will only be very approximate
but it could lead to some interesting discussion and estimation.

   Let the children estimate and weigh some items of clothing from the
dressing-up box or store of costumes for the school plays.

8 Mental work

Revise and practise tables by linking these to weight problems:
  - One weighs 5 g. What will seven weigh?
    How do we do it?
  - The set weigh 24 g. Each one weighs 8 g. How many in the set?
    How do we do it? 24 ÷ 8.

**USING THE
CALCULATOR**   Set the children multiplication and division problems to solve on the
calculator. Reinforce repeated addition by setting problems such as:
'How many sets of 20 g in 300 g?' The children enter 20 + 20 + 20 etc.
Ask how many times they press 20 to get to 300. Can they do it another
way?

LINKS WITH THE ENVIRONMENT

- Talk about weight in grams when shopping. Look at the weights of sweets, tins of food, wool, pet foods, meat.
- Nature. Find out the weights of small creatures such as a mouse or a bird. Which is the lightest animal? How heavy are birds' eggs?
- Clothes. How much do our clothes weigh? For example, cardigans and shoes. Choose smaller things to weigh such as socks and gloves (to weigh less than 1 kg at this time).
- Jumble. The 'rag man' used to sort the clothes into wool, cotton etc. and pay according to the weight.

NOTES ON INVESTIGATIONS

Section A

Do the children weigh accurately? Do they appreciate that there may be differences in weight not only because of size but also because of the kind of material, stuffing, etc?

Section B

Do the children make sensible estimates in choosing clothes that weigh about the same as a jumper? Do they consider not only the size of the garment but also the material it is made from?

Section C

Do the children use both colours? Do they adopt a system? Do they realise that the 25 g balls of red wool can be made into packs of 50 g, 100 g, 200 g, 300 g or 400 g, whilst the 40 g balls of yellow can be made into 200 g and 400 g?

Purpose

- To multiply and divide litres and millilitres
- To give practice in problem-solving situations

Materials

Measuring jugs, large plastic litre bottle, funnel, balance scales, metric weights, containers less than 25 ml

Vocabulary

Litre, millilitre, spoonfuls, most, more, less, label, different, bottle, medicine, waste, weight, capacity, altogether

TEACHING POINTS

1 Litre and millilitre

Remind the children that 1 litre is 1000 ml and $\frac{1}{2}$ litre is 500 ml.

2 Drinks

Make a collection of containers that the children might drink from, such as a cup, mug, plastic beaker or small thermos cup. Let the children estimate how much each one holds and arrange them in order of capacity. Then let them measure how much liquid each holds and label them. Was their estimated order accurate?

Collect some empty popular drink containers such as a carton of fruit juice or a can of cola. Let the children measure their capacities using water and check if it is the same as that stated on the labels. Remind them to allow for the fact that they will not be filled right to the brim.

Make a list of the capacity of cups, mugs, cans, etc. The children could then use a calculator and work out about how many millilitres they drink in an average day.

3 Large drink containers

Talk about how we often buy our drinks in large containers for convenience or perhaps economy.

Collect some empty bottles and cartons. Let the children fill them with water to see how much they hold. Funnels will be useful here. Are they filled right to the brim when we buy them? Why not?

Ask the children to look at a litre bottle and estimate how many beakers it will fill. Let them check their estimate by pouring.

4 Very small containers

Can the children suggest things which hold very small amounts of liquid? Examples are measuring spoons, medicine spoons, thimbles. Give them practice in measuring small amounts of liquid.

5 Medicine

Talk about times when children have been ill and have had to take medicine. Can they tell you what it comes in and how we know how much to take? Can they suggest why we need to know how much to take? (It is worth reminding them that they must never drink medicine unless they are given it by an adult.)

Show the children a plastic 5 ml medicine spoon. Put 100 ml of water in an empty medicine bottle (any bottle will do) and ask the children to estimate how many spoonfuls of water that is. Ask one of the children to check the estimate by pouring. Repeat this with other amounts of water.

6 Mental work

Ask the children questions about capacity such as:
'How much is in two 500 ml bottles? four 500 ml bottles?'
'How many 500 ml are in 3 litres?'
'How many 250 ml are in 1 litre?'
'How many 250 ml are in 2 litres?'

7 Games to play

GUESS THE CAPACITY

Let the children work in groups. Show them a large bottle or container and a beaker or cup. Ask each group to estimate how many beakers can be filled from the bottle and write their estimate on a piece of paper so that the other groups cannot see what they have written. Ask one of the children to find out, by pouring, how many beakers the bottle will fill. The group with the nearest estimate scores a point.

MIX AND MATCH

Have a collection of containers and a card for each container with its capacity written on. Mix the cards up and ask a group of children to match each capacity card to its container. The group scores one point for each correct match. Other groups can mix and match the cards, and try to score more points.

USING THE CALCULATOR

Remind the children that 1000 ml is 1 litre. Ask them to try to make 1 litre on their calculator by adding a combination of these amounts: 100 ml, 200 ml, 250 ml, 500 ml. Can they use the constant function and any of the amounts to make 1 litre?
Ask them to make 2 litres, 3 litres and 4 litres in the same way.

LINKS WITH THE ENVIRONMENT

• Humans – why do we need to drink? How long can we go without a drink? What factors affect this? How much do babies' bottles hold?

- Talk about the variety of drinks at home, in cafés, in shops. How much do we drink in a day? How does this compare with countries where there is a water shortage? Why is it important to have clean drinking water? How is our water made safe to drink?
- Favourite drinks.
- Animals – what do animals usually drink? How do some survive in desert conditions? Some animals don't need to drink but get any liquid they need from plants, animals or insects. For example, the grasshopper mouse and the kangaroo rat in the desert.

NOTES ON INVESTIGATIONS

Section A

Do the children think of several containers which hold less than 25 ml? Do they use the appropriate measuring cylinder to find the capacities?

Section B

Do the children use the fact that 2 spoonfuls hold 10 ml?
2 spoonfuls a day (10 ml) – the medicine will last 12 days,
2 × 2 spoonfuls a day (20 ml) – the medicine will last 6 days,
4 × 2 spoonfuls a day (40 ml) – the medicine will last 3 days,
and so on.

Section C

Do the children use the weight of 1 litre of water (see question C1) to solve the problem? Do they weigh the empty bottle first and then add water until the total weight increases by 500 g? Can they explain how they did it?

Purpose

- To introduce a.m. and p.m. times

Materials

Paper, paper circles (clock faces would be useful)

Vocabulary

Times, o'clock, before, after, mid-day, halfway between, lunch, tea, hour, time line, midnight, noon, circle, earliest, order, p.m., a.m., hours between, arrows

TEACHING POINTS

1 Introduction

Ask the children about the clocks and watches we see. How many children have watches? What kinds of watches are there – with faces, or digital? Hold up a real clock or a geared clock face. Talk about the hands and the movement round the clock face.

2 Revise o'clock, half past, quarter past, quarter to

Set the hands of the clock to various times, for example, 9 o'clock, and ask what time it shows.

Move the hands to half past 9 and ask the new time, and which way the hands moved (clockwise). How far round the clock did the minute hand move? How many minutes has it passed through?

Remind the children about minutes past and 'to' the hour. Set the hands of the clock to quarter to, quarter past and ask similar questions.

Draw some clock faces on the board and ask children to draw the hands to show various times. Remind them that the hour hand is shorter than the minute hand.

3 Five minute intervals

Remind the children how to tell the time in five minute intervals. Ask them to count in fives up to 60. Talk about minutes past and minutes to the hour.

Charts showing five minute intervals could be displayed.

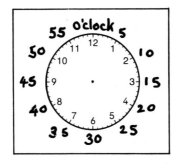 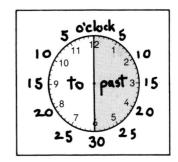

4 Digital time

Talk about the digital notation of time. Remind the children that the minute numbers must always have two digits. The hour numbers may be one or two digits. 9:25 12:35

Many digital clocks display in 24 hours, and some children may notice times like 17:35 or 19:50 .

5 Telling the time

Draw some clock faces on the board or use a teaching clock and talk about the various methods of recording the time.

10 minutes to 3
ten minutes to 3
50 minutes past 2
2:50

Ask the children to stamp some clock faces in their books and record the times in different ways.

A game to play

CLOCK TIMES

Divide the children into two teams. Draw a clock face on the board. Say a time, for example, 'three forty'. Ask a child from the first team to draw in the hands on the clock correctly. Ask a child from the other team to record the time in as many ways as possible. For example, '20 minutes to 4', '40 minutes past 3', '3:40', etc. A point is scored for each way they write it.

This may be done as a group activity.

6 a.m. and p.m.

Talk with the children about the confusion of not knowing whether, say, half past 9 is in the morning or evening. When is it important to know if it is a.m. or p.m.?

Explain that we can show whether a time is in the morning or afternoon by using the letters a.m. and p.m. (a.m. and p.m. stand for the Latin phrases *ante meridiem* and *post meridiem*, meaning before and after mid-day (noon).)

Show a.m. and p.m. on a class time line.

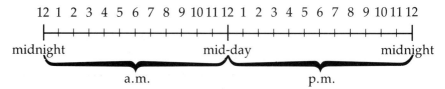

Explain that 12 o'clock at lunchtime is mid-day (the middle of the day or noon) and 12 o'clock at night is midnight (the middle of the night).

Talk about some of the happenings of the day and whether it is a.m. or p.m. For example, get up at 8 o'clock – a.m., set off for school at 8:40 a.m. etc. Show some of these happenings on the time line.

Talk about times like morning, afternoon, evening, lunchtime, tea time, dinner time, supper time and whether they are a.m. or p.m.

7 Clock times using a.m. and p.m.

Ask the children to stamp some clock faces into their books and show some of the important times of their day.

Ask them to record the time and say whether it is a.m. or p.m.

A game to play

A.M. OR P.M.

Play this game with two small groups. Give each group two cards.

a.m.	p.m.

Call out an activity, such as eating breakfast. The first group to hold up the correct card scores a point.

8 Mental work

Ask the children time problems. They have to write the time and say whether it is a.m. or p.m. For example, 'John came in at half past 8, just as the street lamps were switching on. Is this a.m. or p.m.?'

Ask how many hours are between 9 a.m. and 1 p.m. etc.

LINKS WITH THE ENVIRONMENT

- Talk about the types of clocks and watches seen in everyday life. Which have faces and which are digital?
- Make a chart of all the different places clocks can be found.

at home	at school	in the street
alarm clocks	watches	church clock

- Find out how different clocks work – by battery or winding. Make a collection of books about clocks and look at some of the more unusual ones.
- Talk about things that happen during a.m. times, such as delivery of letters or milk, and p.m. times, with street lights coming on, house curtains being closed and children being called in for bed.
- Find out about famous clocks, such as the clock at the Houses of Parliament in London.
- Plan a school trip to a clock museum, or a stately home which will have many different clocks.

NOTES ON INVESTIGATIONS

Section A

Do the children think of things such as going to school at 9 p.m., getting up at 8 p.m., playing out at 2 a.m. in the dark?

Section B

Do the children suggest reasonable times for busy traffic? For example, 8–9 a.m., 12–1 p.m., 5–6 p.m. Do they suggest likely reasons such as people going to work? Do they record their times using a.m. and p.m.?

Section C

Do the children plan an appropriate trip for a school outing? (They may need some help with lengths of journeys. For example, how long it would take to travel to the nearest wildlife park?) Do they show times using a.m. and p.m. notation? Do they allow a reasonable time for meals?

Number 11

Purpose

- To introduce place value of ThHTU
- To introduce addition of ThHTU with 'carrying' from units and from tens
- To introduce subtraction of ThHTU with no decomposition
- To develop number pattern awareness

Materials

Structural apparatus, map of the world

Vocabulary

Thousands, hundreds, tens, units, pounds, number, order, smallest, kilometres, further, distances, journey, chart, longest, shortest, number pattern, pair

TEACHING POINTS

1 Thousands

Talk with the children about places where we might see thousands of people or things.

- Crowds at sports meetings, for example football or rugby, athletics, tennis.
- Fans at a pop concert.
- The number of people living in a town or city. (Do the children know how many people live in their town? This number might be too big for them to cope with at this stage.)
- The number of leaves on a tree
- The number of words in a book
- The number of steps to walk home from school
- The number of minutes in a day

2 Vocabulary

Talk about how numbers are written in words such as thousand, hundred, twenty or seven.

3 Written numbers

Talk about where we see larger numbers written down, for example, car numbers or telephone numbers. Show the children how to write numbers in thousands. Point out that there must always be three digits after the number of thousands.

4 Structural apparatus

Write a number on the board such as 1251 and then use structural apparatus to build this number.

Repeat this activity with children writing four-digit numbers. Let them add the numbers to discover that they arrive at the same starting number.

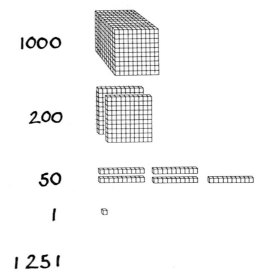

1000

200

50

1

1251

5 Equal numbers

Talk with the children about equal numbers. For example, do they understand that 2000 is 2 thousands, or 20 hundreds, or 200 tens or 2000 units? Structural apparatus is a useful way of showing this.

6 Number values

Ask the children to read numbers and see if they can tell you what each digit is worth. For example, what is the value of the 4 in 2463?

Do they know that three hundred and five is written as 305 and not 35 or 3005?

Give the children practice in putting thousands in order.

It is well worth taking time on these activities to give the children a sound understanding of ThHTU numbers, and the way these are made up.

7 Addition

Addition can be introduced practically using structural apparatus. Write two numbers on the board which use 'carrying' in either the tens or units (but not both), such as 1246 and 1326. Ask one child to add them as a sum on the board and another to add them using structural apparatus.

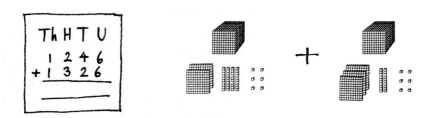

Do they both get the same answer?

8 Subtraction

Show this practically using structural apparatus, taking care to avoid decomposition.

Set out a number like 3354. Ask a child to take 1223 away from it using the apparatus. Then write down the number left.

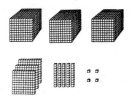

Ask another child to work out the answer in a different way, in their head or with a calculator perhaps.

Are the answers the same?

9 Lists or tables

Give the children experience in reading numbers from lists or tables showing large numbers such as heights of mountains, lengths of rivers or traffic surveys.

10 Mental work

- For practice in place value, give the children a number such as 400. Ask them to say and write a thousands number with it in, for example 2476.
- Practise counting on in thousands. 1200, 2200, 3200, . . . , 8200.
- Give practice in counting back in thousands. 8500, 7500, . . . , 1500.
- Ask the children to tell you what the tens digits are worth in different numbers you say or write.
- Give practice in adding and subtracting hundreds and tens. For example, 600 + 2 hundreds or 40 − 3 tens.
- Ask the children addition and subtraction questions in problem situations.

11 Games to play

MAKE A NUMBER

Working in pairs, the children take turns to make a thousand number using structural apparatus. They write the number on a piece of paper and turn it over so that their friend cannot see it. The friend counts the apparatus, writes the number down and then they compare answers. If they both get it right, they each score a point. If their answers differ they ask the teacher which one is correct, and whoever gave the correct answer gets the point.

MISSING NUMBERS

Write a number on the board, for example 6754. Ask a child to make it using structural apparatus. That child then hides their eyes or turns their back. Another child then removes one or two pieces. The first child works out what is missing by looking at the original number on the board and by checking the pieces. They say how much was taken away and write the new number on the board.

HUNDREDS AND TENS BINGO

This game can be played with two groups of four children. Make a simple 'bingo' card for each group using thousands numbers, but don't use the same digit twice in the tens or the hundreds. Make a small card for each hundreds and tens number on the bingo cards and put all the cards in a bag. Shake them up and then ask a child to pick them out one at a time. If the group can use the card they claim it and put it on the relevant bingo card number. If $\boxed{400}$ was picked up it could be put on $\boxed{4462}$. The group to cover their bingo card first wins.

1256	4462
3972	5139

$\boxed{200}$ $\boxed{50}$ $\boxed{900}$ $\boxed{70}$

$\boxed{400}$ $\boxed{60}$ $\boxed{100}$ $\boxed{30}$

USING THE CALCULATOR   Number patterns.

- Ask the children to make number patterns on their calculators using the constant function or continuous addition.

10, 20, . . . , 90, 100
100, 200, 300, . . . , 1000
Ask them to count back using the calculator again using the
constant function or continuous subtraction.
1000, 900, 800, . . . , 100
100, 90, 80, . . . , 10
9, 8, . . . , 1

- Add or subtract hundreds to a number to make patterns. For
  example 1240, 1340, . . . or 3927, 3827, . . .
- Give the children plenty of practice in showing thousands
  numbers on the calculator and observing how these are
  displayed. Call out a number like 7843. Ask them to show it on
  their displays, then hold the calculator up so that it can be
  checked. Can other children read the number on the display?

LINKS WITH THE ENVIRONMENT

Talk about where we can see or use four-digit numbers in everyday
life. These include

- Dates in history linking with various events like 1066 and the
  Battle of Hastings or 1666 and the Great Fire of London
- Populations of small towns and villages
- Distances travelled. Ask the children how far they have
  travelled. Has anyone travelled more than 1000 kilometres or
  miles?
- Telephone numbers. Has anyone a four-digit telephone
  number? If so, can they read it in words?

NOTES ON INVESTIGATIONS

Section A

Do the children appreciate place value? Do they devise a system for
finding all the possible answers?

1   10   11
100   101   110   111
1000   1001   1010   1011   1100   1101   1110   1111

Section B

Do the children appreciate that the distance from A to C must be the
same as the distance from A to B and from B to C together? Do they
choose realistic distances for an aeroplane flight? Do any children
choose a distance from A to B or B to C and subtract it from 8999 to find
the other distance?

Section C

Do the children understand how to use the chart and choose a suitable city? Do they visit three other destinations and keep the total less than 10 000 km? Do they relate their choice to their knowledge of the world map – are the places reasonably close to each other?

Angles 2

Purpose

- To introduce the half right angle and 45°
- To introduce the eight points of the compass

Materials

Compass, card and paper fasteners (these will be useful to make compass pointers)

Vocabulary

Right angle, compass points, map, half right angle, shape, directions, north, south, east, west, north-west, north-east, south-east, south-west, middle, shorter, trail, degrees

TEACHING POINTS

1 Making a right angle

Remind the children that a square corner is also a right angle. Ask them to make one by folding a piece of paper.

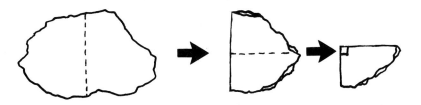

Ask them to look for right angles around the room.

2 Four points of the compass

Talk about the compass and ask what it is used for. What are the four main compass points called?

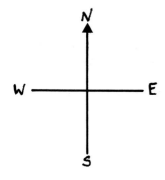

Draw a compass on the board. Remind the children that the angles between the four points of the compass are right angles or 90° each and that we pass through four right angles when we turn through all four points of the compass.

3 Half right angles and 45°

Ask the children to fold a sheet of paper to make a $\frac{1}{2}$ right angle. Ask how many $\frac{1}{2}$ right angles are in one right angle, and how many degrees there are in a $\frac{1}{2}$ right angle (45°).

Ask the children to look for right angles in the room and use their 45° angles to find out how many fit into a right angle.

4 Eight points of the compass

Talk about the $\frac{1}{2}$ right angle and the eight points of the compass. Show the children how to use their paper $\frac{1}{2}$ right angle to count the $\frac{1}{2}$ right angles as they go right round a compass.

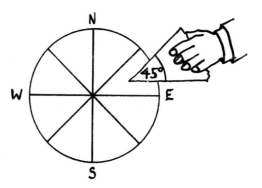

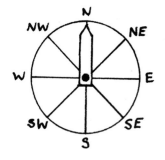

The point or direction between north and east is north-east. What are the other points called? Help the children to build up the eight points and make a small card compass using a card pointer and a paper fastener.

Give the children practice in using their compass by asking such questions as:

'How many $\frac{1}{2}$ right angles are there between south and west?'

'How many $\frac{1}{2}$ right angles are there between north-west and south-east?'

5 The 45° angle

Ask the children to draw the eight points of the compass on squared paper, using a ruler, and to make each line into a petal shape.

Ask the children to colour each petal:
'Colour the south-east petal green. Go 45° clockwise from north and colour that petal red.'
Continue the instructions until all the petals are coloured.

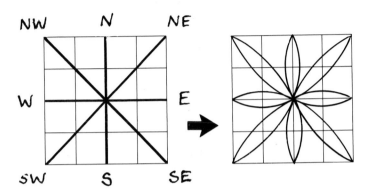

6 In the classroom

Mark the eight points of the compass on the walls of the room as accurately as possible. Ask the children to face various directions, and to say what they see. A simple class plan can be drawn.

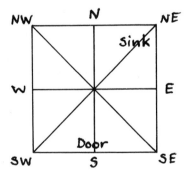

Ask how many $\frac{1}{2}$ right angles they pass through as they move from one direction to another. Use the card compass from activity 4.

7 Following directions

Draw a square grid on the board. Let the children give you the directions for drawing a trail or pattern on the grid using the eight points of the compass.

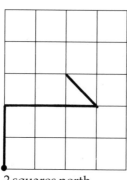

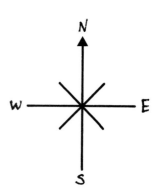

2 squares north,
3 squares east,
1 square north-west . . .

Give children squared paper and a starting point. Call out directions for them to draw a shape, such as 'Go north 3 squares' for starting.

Games to play

FIND THE MISSING ANIMAL

Use squared paper and mark the starting point X. Ask the children to draw lines with a ruler.

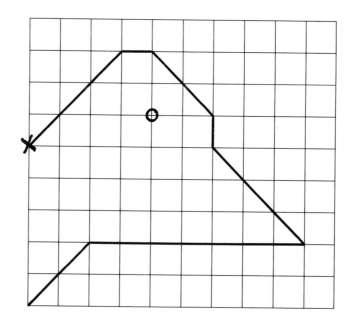

1. Move across 3 squares NE   5. Across 3 squares SE
2. 1 square E   6. 7 squares W
3. Across 2 squares SE   7. Across 2 squares SW
4. 1 square S

Add an eye to make it more realistic.

TREASURE MAPS

Ask the children to draw an island on squared paper and plan three moves from a landing spot to reach the treasure. This spot may be given by the teacher or the children can decide it for a friend to find.

This map may also be used to develop a story:
'The explorers landed, travelled NW and made camp for the night. They went . . . and saw the . . .'

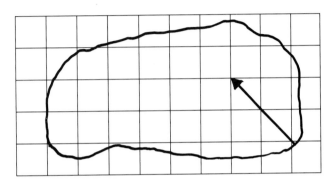

8 The British Isles

In preparation for the work in sections B and C it is helpful for the children to look at a map of the British Isles to find where they live and also the main cities.

LINKS WITH THE ENVIRONMENT

Talk about everyday situations involving compass directions.

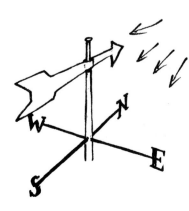

- Maps. Use maps of Britain and the world to find positions of towns, cities and countries.
- Walking and hiking. Discuss how hikers follow directions and use a compass.
- Flying and sailing.
- Talk about the use of a compass and the instruments used today.
- History. How did the ancient travellers find their way? (Stars, sun, etc.)
- Towns and street plans. Following directions on the local map.
- Weather vanes. Are there any weather vanes on local buildings? Look at the different designs. The 'tail' is larger than the 'head' in order to catch the wind. Ask the children to explain how a weather vane works. Note that a north wind blows *from* the north and that the weather vane points to the direction the wind is blowing from.

**NOTES ON
INVESTIGATIONS**

Section A

An introduction to the use of the compass may be necessary for some children. Do they realise that the compass needle always points to the north? Can they identify the directions of places in school from the classroom? Perhaps the hall or cloakroom are north from the classroom.

It is helpful to decide where the compass is going to be placed and for a simple sketch plan of the school to be drawn on the board and the points of the compass marked.

This investigation may also be done in the school hall, and is especially useful when done with a class or large group.

Section B

Do the children look carefully at the map of the British Isles and give clear and accurate instructions?

Section C

Do the children choose a town that gives plenty of scope for different directions? Do they choose towns or cities near to where they live? Do they see the significance of giving directions *from* other places to the chosen town? Are they accurate with their directions?

This investigation could be extended as a group or class activity.

Purpose

- To introduce subtraction of HTU with decomposition from hundreds and tens
- To revise place value of thousands, hundreds, tens and units
- To develop addition and subtraction strategies
- To introduce negative numbers

Materials

Structural apparatus as required, calculator

Vocabulary

Thousands, hundreds, tens, units, take away, order, smallest, odd, add, largest, even, subtract, patterns, digit, circle, zero, nearest thousand, puzzles, subtracting, between, calculator, number, shape, down, across

TEACHING POINTS   **1 Numbers**

Talk with the children about numbers generally and ask questions related to different numbers and patterns.

'Where can different numbers be spotted?' – bus numbers, house numbers, car numbers, telephone numbers.

'What kinds of patterns do numbers have?' – odd, even, pattern of 2, 5, 10 etc.

'Where are odd and even numbers found?'

'Where will there be large numbers of people?' – football and rugby matches, concerts, in a school, airport, carnivals.

'Where can you find large numbers of objects?' – tins in a supermarket, apples on a market stall, a lorry load of potatoes, books in a shop.

'Where do numbers end? Do they go on for ever? This is called infinity.'

2 Revise place value of thousands, hundreds, tens and units

Talk with the children about place value and large numbers. Write a large number on the board and ask the children to read the number. Can they say what each digit is worth?

2 units = 2
5 tens = 50
3 hundreds = 300
1 thousand = 1000

This could be shown in different ways. How many ways can the children find to show a number? These are some possible variations.

- as an abacus

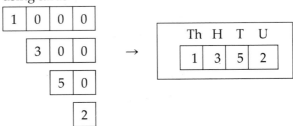

- using cards

1	0	0	0

	3	0	0

→

Th	H	T	U
1	3	5	2

		5	0

			2

- using structural apparatus

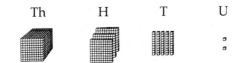

Th   H   T   U

- pencil and paper methods

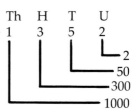

Th	H	T	U
1	3	5	2

└ 2
└ 50
└ 300
└ 1000

- calculator

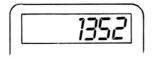

Talk with the children about numbers where the digits are the same, like 3333. Point to two of the 3s – for example the units and the tens 3s – and ask how many times larger the tens 3 is than the units 3. Do this for the other 3s and find a pattern. Practise this with other identical-digit numbers.

Write a number with different digits such as 1357. Ask a child to write a number that is larger than 1357 but less than 2000. Ask others to write even larger numbers but still less than 2000. Try varying this activity, for example, by asking for an odd number smaller than 1357, or for some large numbers in order.

Let the children practise writing numbers. Ask one child to write 708 on the board. Ask others to write the numbers which follow. Watch out that 710 is not written as 7010 – do the children know why 7010 is not the same as 710? Repeat the activity with numbers involving ThHTU, for example, 7000, 7009, 7010.

3 Games to play

KEEP THE PATTERN GOING

start 1000

add 200
each time

Play this game in small teams. Decide on a starting number and a number pattern. Players from each team take turns to write the next number in the pattern. One point is scored for each correct number. The game ends when each child has had a turn, and the team with the most points are declared the winners.

ADD OR TAKE

Put a selection of addition and subtraction cards in a box, for example,

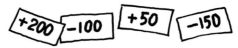

Write a number on the board and let the children in turn pick a number from the box and write a new number on the board.

Beware of the likelihood of reaching negative numbers. If the children aren't ready for these it may be advisable to stop the game and start again with a new thousands number. This is also a game to introduce or reinforce negative numbers.

4 Mental work – addition and subtraction strategies

Some of the following activities can be introduced in oral or written form, and sometimes as word problems.

- Add $9 + 9 + 9$ $(10 + 10 + 10 - 3)$
- Add $99 + 99 + 99$ $(100 + 100 + 100 - 3)$
- Add numbers by adding the tens digit
  $50 + 50$ $70 + 70$ $90 + 90 + 90$ $60 + 60 + 60 + 60$
- Add several numbers by first matching up pairs of digits which add up to 10.

$$
\begin{array}{c}
3 \\ 4 \\ + 7 \\ \hline -
\end{array}
\qquad
\begin{array}{c}
5 \\ 2 \\ + 5 \\ \hline -
\end{array}
\qquad
\begin{array}{c}
6 \\ 4 \\ + 7 \\ \hline -
\end{array}
\qquad
\begin{array}{c}
1 \\ 8 \\ + 9 \\ \hline -
\end{array}
\qquad
\begin{array}{c}
7 \\ 2 \\ 3 \\ + 8 \\ \hline -
\end{array}
$$

- Link addition and subtraction by writing number bonds.

  5, 9 and 14 $\rightarrow$ $5 + 9 = 14$ $14 - 9 = 5$
  $\qquad\qquad\qquad\quad$ $9 + 5 = 14$ $14 - 5 = 9$

- Practise linking addition and subtraction by finding missing numbers.

$$
\begin{array}{c}
\square \\ - 9 \\ \hline 5
\end{array}
\qquad
\begin{array}{c}
\square \\ - 5 \\ \hline 9
\end{array}
\qquad
\begin{array}{c}
\square \\ - 15 \\ \hline 4
\end{array}
\qquad
\begin{array}{c}
\square \\ - 12 \\ \hline 26
\end{array}
$$

- Check subtractions by adding . This helps children realise that addition and subtraction are related.

$$
\begin{array}{c}
48 \\ - 26 \\ \hline 22
\end{array}
\qquad
\begin{array}{c}
26 \\ + 22 \\ \hline 48
\end{array}
\qquad
\begin{array}{c}
152 \\ - 29 \\ \hline 123
\end{array}
\qquad
\begin{array}{c}
123 \\ + 29 \\ \hline 152
\end{array}
$$

- Ask word problems involving addition and subtraction. For example, four hundred and thirty people were in a plane. One hundred were children. How many were adults?

```
H T U
3 4 2
− 1 9 5
───────
```

5 Subtraction of HTU with decomposition from the hundreds and tens

Structural apparatus is one way of visually showing the decomposition method.

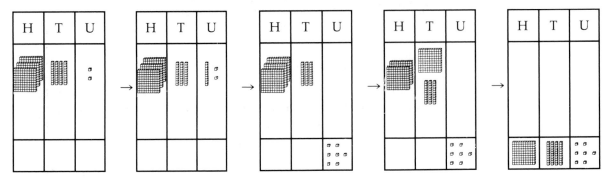

Talk about the method of recording this, although you may have other preferred methods. Let children work out their own algorithms for recording.

$$
\begin{array}{r}
\text{H T U} \\
3.\ 4\ 2 \\
-\ 1\ 9\ 5 \\
\hline
\end{array}
\qquad
\begin{array}{r}
\text{H T U} \\
{}^{2}3^{13}4\ {}^{1}2 \\
-\ 1\ 9\ 5 \\
\hline
1\ 4\ 7
\end{array}
$$

Give the children plenty of practice with decomposition.

6 Negative numbers

Talk with the children about negative whole numbers. Use the constant function on a calculator to count back in ones from 10 until they reach 0. Ask them to continue the subtraction pattern and see what happens on the display.

$$10\ 9\ 8\ 7\ 6\ 5\ 4\ 3\ 2\ 1\ 0 \rightarrow -1\ -2\ -3$$

Use a number line to explain what is happening.

$$-5\ -4\ -3\ -2\ -1\ \ 0\ \ 1\ \ 2\ \ 3\ \ 4\ \ 5$$

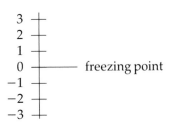

Repeat this with other starting numbers and subtraction patterns. Negative numbers are seen when the temperature is below freezing. Talk about the temperatures in winter and summer. Show the children a thermometer marked in Celsius and let them read the marks. Ask them what happens on the thermometer when the weather is very cold. The thermometer will show negative numbers. Draw a picture to show this.

Depending on the time of year, ask them to watch the weather forecast on the television and to notice if any of the temperatures are below zero. They can also look in the newspaper to see the temperatures in Britain and in other parts of the world. They might be interested to compare the temperatures of some of the coldest places like Siberia or Antarctica. They can investigate places with temperatures below freezing while it is summer in Britain.

7 Rounding up and down

Talk about rounding numbers to the nearest hundred. Remind them that 50 or more rounds up to the next hundred, and less than 50 is rounded down. For example,

$451 \to 500 \quad 623 \to 600 \quad 849 \to 800 \quad 350 \to 400.$

Ask them to round larger numbers to the nearest thousand and talk about how useful this is in estimating answers.

$6384 \to 6000 \quad 4871 \to 5000 \quad 2706 \to 3000$

USING THE CALCULATOR

Check that the children know how to use the calculator for subtraction involving HTU.

Use the calculator for work on place value involving ThTHU. Enter a number such as 299 or 999 and ask the children what will happen when 1 is added each time. Ask them to add or subtract in 10s, 100s or 1000s to reinforce number patterns and place value. For example,

352   452   552   652   752   852   952   1052 . . .

1325   1315   1305   1295   1285 . . .

Use the calculator for negative number patterns and watch what happens to the display.

A game to play

SHOOT TO ZERO

Two children play using one calculator. One child enters a four-digit number such as 2941. The second child has to reduce the number to 0 with only four subtractions. For example,

2941 − 900
2041 − 40
2001 − 1
2000 − 2000

The children then change over.

LINKS WITH THE ENVIRONMENT   Talk with the children about everyday situations involving addition and subtraction of large numbers. These might include:

- subtracting from 301 or 501 in a game of darts
- the number of shopping days to Christmas
- the number of people attending school concerts over several days and the total number of tickets or programmes sold

The weather forecast on television and weather patterns elsewhere in the world sometimes give negative temperatures.

NOTES ON INVESTIGATIONS

Section A

Do the children understand that number patterns continue when negative numbers are involved? Do their patterns all involve negative numbers? Do any children start at zero and count down?

Section B

Do the children write appropriate clues for finding their mystery number? Do the clues only give one mystery number out of the group of numbers? Are the other numbers chosen so that it is not too obvious which is the mystery number?

Section C

Do the children use number patterns for finding numbers to fit in the circles? For example, 143, 144, 145, 146, 147. Do they realise that the numbers 143 and 147 and the numbers 144, 146 give the same total?

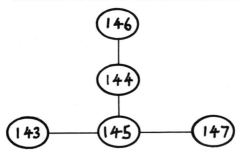

Do they find other solutions that work?

shape 3

Purpose

- To introduce the concept of a net
- To introduce the nets of the cube and cuboid
- To give children practice in constructing other nets

Materials

2 cm squared paper, 1 cm squared paper, scissors, sticky tape, templates for equilateral triangles, attractive boxes of various shapes for display, boxes suitable for opening out to make nets

Vocabulary

Cube, cuboid, pyramid, tetrahedron, box, shape, net, large, squares, different, opposite faces, equilateral triangle, template, fit inside

TEACHING POINTS

1 Gift boxes

Talk about gift and chocolate boxes and how they are made. Show the children one of the flat gift boxes that can be bought at a stationers and how it opens up into a box. Make a collection of different shaped fancy boxes. Talk about how they are decorated and how some have lids attached.

2 Solid shapes

Talk about the more familiar solid shapes that are used for boxes, for example, the cube, cuboid, pyramid, tetrahedron, triangular prism, hexagonal prism and cylinder. For each box ask the children how many faces it has. What are the shapes of the faces? How many corners (vertices) has each one?

Ask them to sort the boxes in different ways, according to the number of faces or vertices, or any other criteria.

3 Nets

Introduce the idea of nets by taking a cuboid box apart and laying it flat.

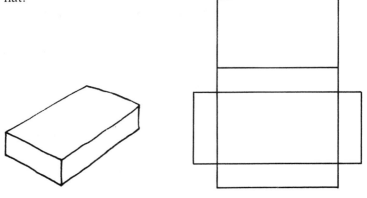

Let a child try to fold it into a box again. Do this with several boxes to show that each one has a net. Don't worry about overlapping tabs at this point. If it will confuse the children then cut them off.

Find similar boxes that can be shown to have different nets.

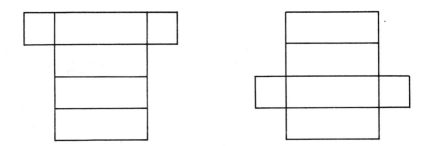

4 Make a box

Make a box as a class activity. Draw the net for a cuboid on large squared paper. Cut it out and then show the children how they can use a ruler to help them fold the edges neatly.

Ask one child to fold the net into a cuboid. Either hold the sides together or use sticky tape to make the shape. Let the child describe the box saying how many faces it has, and the shape of each face.

5 Other boxes

Look at other boxes or containers that are not cuboids. Show how these open or split up. Talk about the shapes they are made from.

6 An unexpected result

Show the children a toilet roll tube and ask them to name the shape. Unroll it and show how it is made. Children often expect a toilet roll tube to give a rectangle whereas it gives a parallelogram. Does this also apply to other tubes?

 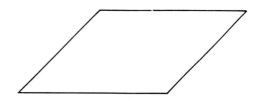

7 Games to play

SPEEDY BOX

Provide a selection of nets for boxes. Let two children race to pick up a net each and make it into a box using sticky tape. The winner is the first to complete a box.

FAST MATCH

In an open box put a selection of boxes. The children will need to be familiar with their nets. For each box, draw its net on a piece of card. Put the cards into the open box.

Let children time how long it takes them to match each box with its net. If the boxes and cards are numbered then the children can check if their responses are correct. Let them see if they can repeat the activity in a faster time.

LINKS WITH THE ENVIRONMENT

- Look at unusual boxes from shops and discuss what their nets might look like.
- Make some boxes in Craft and decorate them. They can be used for gifts.

money box   paper weight

- Look around school and home for cardboard containers. Investigate their nets.
- Talk about how to design boxes for special things, like toys, chocolates, jewellery, notelets.
- Think about how boxes are made and stored before being filled.

**NOTES ON
INVESTIGATIONS**

Section A

Do the children draw different shapes using five squares
(pentominoes)? Do they find that some shapes will make a box
without a lid and some won't?

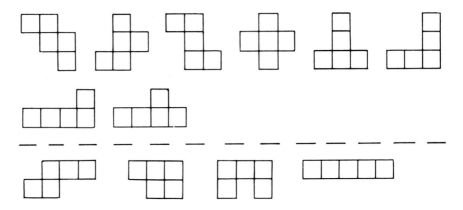

Section B

Do the children understand that a box can have different shapes for its
net depending on how it is cut?

Section C

Do the children draw and make the nets of cubes or cuboids? Do any
children make other shapes, such as pyramids? Do the boxes fit inside
each other?

Number 13

Purpose

- To use a multiplication square up to 10 × 10
- To develop an awareness of number pattern
- Multiplication of two digits by one digit with answers in HTU
- To introduce factors of numbers

Materials

Individual multiplication squares, crayons or felt tip pens, calculators

Vocabulary

Multiplication square, factors, tables, odd numbers, patterns, notice,
diagram, circle, opposite numbers, multiply, pairs, corner numbers,
larger

TEACHING POINTS

1 Make a multiplication square

Make a multiplication square, perhaps a large one as a class activity, to help the children fully understand how to use it. Fill it in table by table.

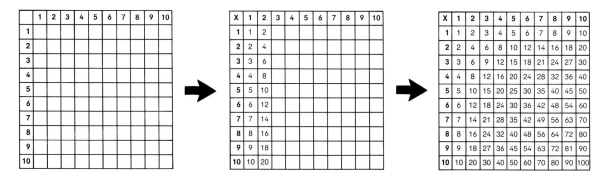

2 Using a multiplication square

Show the children how to use a multiplication square to multiply two numbers.

Give the children individual multiplication squares (the squares will last longer if they are mounted on card). Let the children practise using them to find answers to multiplication questions.

Make multiplication flash cards. Hold them up and ask the children to use their squares to find the answers.

3 Factors

Talk about factors, and explain, for example, that 4 and 3 are factors of 12.

Show the children how to find the factors of any number on the multiplication square. Let them choose a number and follow the horizontal and vertical lines from that number to find its factors.

Give the children practice in finding factors of different numbers on the class grid. Ask them to find the factors of 24. Then ask them to find another 24 on the square. What are the different factors now? How many pairs of factors can they find for 24? What other numbers are there with several pairs of factors?

4 Recording multiplication

Talk with the children about recording multiplication. This is one way, although you may prefer another; children can also devise their own algorithm.

$$\begin{array}{r} 39 \\ \times 5 \\ \hline 195 \\ \hline 4 \end{array}$$

5 Games to play

HUNT THE FACTORS

Choose two teams and give each player a multiplication square. Write a number from the square on the board, for example, 24. Ask the first player of one team to give as many pairs of factors of that number as they can. They score a point for each pair of factors. Write another number on the board with an equivalent number of factors. The first player of the second team finds all the factors for that number. If the children are finding this too easy, let them play without the aid of the multiplication square or set a time limit for each answer.

FIND THE NUMBER

This is an alternative to HUNT THE FACTORS. This time the children are given the factors and are asked to find the number they make. For example, 3 and 8 are the factors, what is the number?

STAND UP FACTORS

Give 10 children one card each with a number on it (1–10). Call out a multiple, for example 14. Any children holding the factors of 14 must hold up their cards. Anyone failing to do so is out and hands their card to a new player.

6 Function machines

Talk about simple function machines.

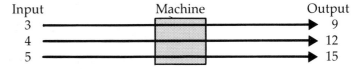

Input	Machine	Output
3		9
4		12
5		15

Ask what happens to the left-hand number to get the number on the right-hand side. What is the function?

Give the children practice in putting numbers in different multiplication machines. For example

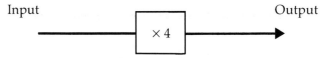

Input   Output
                        × 4

Can they explain what is happening?

7 Mental Work

- Let the children practise with their multiplication tables. Devise a variety of games and activities to make this enjoyable.

Games to play

SNAP

Make two piles of cards. One pile will have multiplication sentences on them and the other will have the answers. Players call 'snap' when the sentence matches the answer.

PAIRS

Use the SNAP cards to play PAIRS. Turn the cards face down and shuffle them around. Players take turns to pick up two cards to see if they make a pair.

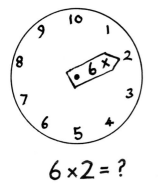

6 × 2 = ?

TABLES SPINNER

Make a spinner with the numbers 1–10 around the edge.
Children take turns to spin the arrow and have to say the answer to the multiplication. If their answer is correct they can collect a counter. The winner can be the one with the most counters after a specified time.

- Ask the children to find missing numbers like this,

  $4 \times \square = 12$

- Ask the children questions about factors. Devise a factor quiz where children need to work out the answers to questions within a specified time; questions like,
  'What are the factors of twelve?'
  'What is the number if the factors are three and five?'
- Ask the children to find the missing numbers in patterns. For example,

  5   10   15   20   –   –   –   40.

- Give the children mental problems to solve using their multiplication square. For example, if they spend about 6 hours a day at school, how many hours a week is this? Or ask them how many days are in 7 full weeks.

USING THE CALCULATOR

Use the constant function to make number patterns.

A game to play

FINDING FACTORS

Give two children the same factors, for example 8 and 3. The first person to find the number using their calculator scores one point. The winner is the first to score 10 points. This can also be done as a mental activity, or made more difficult by using larger numbers.

Section A

Do the children find that some of the colours coincide? Do they realise that this is because 2 and 4 are factors of 8?

Section B

Do the children realise that any number will have one pair of factors as a number can always be multiplied by 1? Any number that is not a prime number will have at least two pairs of factors, the factors pairs for 6 are 1, 6 and 2, 3. Some have three or more pairs, like 12 which has 1, 12 and 3, 4 and 2, 6.

Section C

Do they choose other 2 by 2 squares on the multiplication table? Do they choose 3 by 3 squares? Do they discover that the relationship is the same for any size square on the multiplication square? For example,

1	2
2	4

$1 \times 4 = 4$

$2 \times 2 = 4$

5	6	7
10	12	14
15	18	21

$5 \times 21 = 105$

$7 \times 15 = 105$

6	8	10	12
9	12	15	18
12	16	20	24
15	20	25	30

$6 \times 30 = 180$

$12 \times 15 = 180$

Purpose

- To revise the half square method for finding area
- To draw and find the area of shapes using cm^2

Materials

Squared paper, tracing paper, plain paper or card, transparent grid

Vocabulary

Area, estimate, total, twice, different, fold, half, difference between, squared paper, square centimetre (cm^2)

TEACHING POINTS

1 Recording area

Remind the children that area is the amount of surface covered by a shape.

   Draw a rectangular shape on the board. Ask them to find its area. Remind them that the standard unit for measuring area is the square centimetre, written as cm^2.

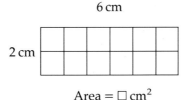

6 cm

2 cm

This shape has an area of 12 cm^2

Area = □ cm^2

2 The half square method for finding area

Remind the children about this method of counting squares and half squares. It is especially useful for finding the areas of irregular shapes.

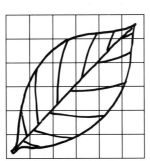
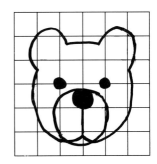

Let the children practise finding different areas. Draw shapes on squared paper. First ask the children to estimate each area. Then remind them how to find the approximate area using the half square method.

- Count all the whole squares first
- Count half squares, or greater, as whole squares
- Don't count anything less than half a square

Children may find it helpful to mark with a dot the squares they have already counted.

Remind them that if the shape is drawn on 1 cm squared paper the area is written in square centimetres.

3 Hands

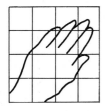

Ask the children to draw round their closed hands on squared paper. Ask them to estimate the area and then let them find it by using the half square method. Write the area of each hand.

Talk about the estimates and how close they were to the actual areas.

Cut out the paper hands and display them so that the children can compare the areas of their hands. The results can also be shown on a graph, and it is also interesting to compare the areas of their feet in the same way.

4 Using a grid sheet

Show the children how to use a transparent cm^2 grid sheet or one marked on tracing paper. Ask them to draw a picture on plain paper, estimate the picture's area first and then find its area using the grid sheet.

5 Drawing activities

Ask the children to work in pairs and each to draw a picture on 1 cm squared paper. The picture needs to be a simple line drawing and not too complicated. Each child estimates the area of both pictures and then checks by counting to see who made the closer estimate.

6 Conservation activities

Ask each child to draw a different picture with a 'fixed' area, for example, 45 cm^2. These 'fixed' area pictures could be displayed and used to talk about the conservation of area.

For another activity the children could draw a rectangle on 1 cm squared paper and find its area. They could then draw and cut this rectangle into different pieces and rearrange them to form a new shape.

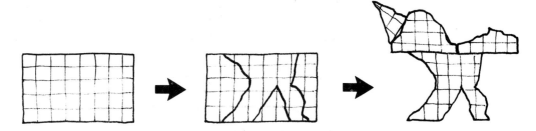

Now count the area of the rearranged shape. What do they find about the two areas?

A game to play

MATCH THE AREA

Make two identical sets of eight cards; draw shapes on a 1 cm² grid on four cards and write the areas on the other four.

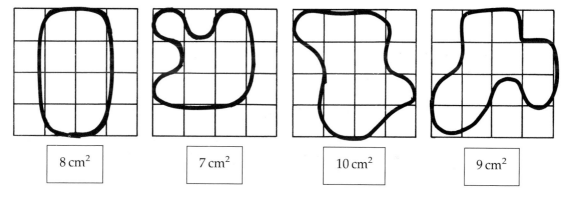

8 cm²	7 cm²	10 cm²	9 cm²

Give one complete set to each of two small groups of children. Ask them to match the area cards to the shapes by counting using the half square method. The group to do it first wins.

LINKS WITH THE ENVIRONMENT

- Talk with the children about where we might see areas in square centimetres – graph paper, some mosaic pictures and patterns.
- Make a collection of leaves. Compare the area of a leaf when it is still fresh and when it dries and withers, and the areas of leaves from different trees.
- Which tree in the school grounds has leaves with the biggest area?
- Make a collection of brass rubbings of objects and find their areas.

- Make a collection of pictures with a common theme, for example snooker players or animals. Cut the pictures from newspapers or magazines and compare their areas using a grid. It makes an interesting activity to compare which newspaper gives the greater coverage following a popular event.
- Silhouettes of heads could be measured in cm² and displayed. To draw the silhouette of a head, draw the outline of a shadow on a piece of paper on the wall. The area can be measured using a transparent grid, or the silhouette drawn directly onto squared paper. Make sure the children understand that this is **not** the area of a head!

NOTES ON INVESTIGATIONS

Section A

Do the children draw leaves of reasonable size? Do the children draw and carefully count the squares on the first leaf using the half square method? Do they then count and mark the matching number of squares to be covered by the second leaf before drawing it? Do they put dots to help them count? Do they then draw the second leaf outline round the dotted squares to match the area they have counted out? Do they remember that if they include any extra squares in their outline they must be less then $\frac{1}{2}$ square each or the total will be wrong?

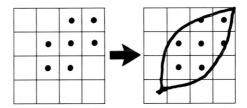

Some children may use a trial and error approach. For example, some may draw the leaves first and then count the squares hoping they will both be the same area. Talk with them about the difficulty of this.

Section B

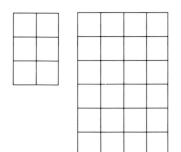

How do the children draw the leaf twice the size? Do they realise that if the first leaf is on a 2 by 3 grid, the second one is on a 4 by 6 grid, and that the area of the larger leaf is four times as big?
Do they try it for other leaf shapes and find the same relationship? If they don't, can they say why? Talk about the problems of enlarging the leaf accurately.
This investigation should lead to some interesting discussion.
A simpler form of this activity is to enlarge a rectangle rather than a leaf.

Section C

Do the children realise that the five leaves are not all the same size? Do they divide 45 by 5 to begin with and then allow for different sizes when deciding on the area of each leaf to fit the picture? Do they work it out like this on paper or with a calculator?

$$45 \, \text{cm}^2 \div 5 = 9 \, \text{cm}^2$$
$$9 \, \text{cm}^2 + 9 \, \text{cm}^2 + 9 \, \text{cm}^2 + 9 \, \text{cm}^2 + 9 \, \text{cm}^2 = 45 \, \text{cm}^2$$
$$6 \, \text{cm}^2 + 6 \, \text{cm}^2 + 9 \, \text{cm}^2 + 9 \, \text{cm}^2 + 15 \, \text{cm}^2 = 45 \, \text{cm}^2$$

Do they draw the leaves by marking the number of dots for the leaves and then drawing the outline around them?

Number 14

Purpose

- To introduce division of hundreds, tens and units by one digit

Materials

Squared paper, structural apparatus, calculator

Vocabulary

Double, divide, divide exactly, cross-number puzzle, share, answer, digits, pairs, groups, larger, add, calculator, across, down

TEACHING POINTS   **1 Division patterns**

Talk with the children about division and the different ways of recording it. These are some possible ways.

$$8 \div 2 = 4 \qquad 2 \overline{)8}^{\,4} \qquad \tfrac{8}{2} = 4$$

Remind them that we can show division patterns by grouping the numbers in 2s, 3s, 4s, etc. Talk about these patterns and draw some of them or ask the children to make them using squared paper.

1	2
3	4
5	6
7	8
9	10
11	12
13	14
15	16
17	18
19	20

1	2	3
4	5	6
7	8	9
10	11	12
13	14	15
16	17	18
19	20	21
22	23	24
25	26	27
28	29	30

1	2	3	4
5	6	7	8
9	10	11	12
13	14	15	16
17	18	19	20
21	22	23	24
25	26	27	28
29	30	31	32
33	34	35	36
37	38	39	40

1	2	3	4	5
6	7	8	9	10
11	12	13	14	15
16	17	18	19	20
21	22	23	24	25
26	27	28	29	30
31	32	33	34	35
36	37	38	39	40
41	42	43	44	45
46	47	48	49	50

Make a display of the patterns and use them to ask questions like 'How many 2s in 14?'

Talk about the number patterns and ask the children to count in 2s, 3s, 4s, etc.

2 Link multiplication and division

Explain that multiplication and division are related. Write three numbers linked by multiplication and division, for example, 2, 5, 10. This can be shown using squared paper.

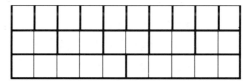

Ask the children to write multiplication and division bonds for them.

$$2 \times 5 = 10 \qquad 10 \div 2 = 5$$
$$5 \times 2 = 10 \qquad 10 \div 5 = 2$$

Do this for other numbers. Ask the children to use multiplication and division to check answers. For example if $20 \div 4 = 5$ then $4 \times 5 = 20$.

3 Revise division of tens and units by one digit

Use structural apparatus to show what is happening.

Use your usual words to explain that we are sharing the number into two equal groups. Talk about the method of writing this down. This is one possible way, but the children may prefer to devise their own algorithms.

$$\begin{array}{r} 1\,7 \\ 2\,\overline{)\,3\,^1 4} \end{array}$$

4 Division of hundreds, tens and units by one digit

Use structural apparatus for showing this to give the children imagery, and talk about the mothod of recording.

Structural apparatus can also be used to show division with 'carrying', this imagery will help the children to understand or devise a method of recording.

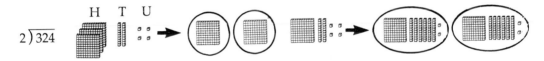

5 Mental work

- Give the children practice in using both multiplication and division bonds up to 10×10.

  $20 \div 2 = \square$ $20 \div 10 = \square$ $2 \times 10 = \square$ $10 \times 2 = \square$
  $20 \div \square = 10$ $20 \div \square = 2$

- Ask the children division problems.
  'Twelve children sit in double seats; how many seats do they need?'
  'Peter has the same hours of sleep each night. If he has 56 hours of sleep in one week, how many hours of sleep will he have each night?'
  'There are 153 children travelling on 3 coaches. How many would there be on one coach if there were the same number on each?'

USING THE CALCULATOR   Let the children practise division by one digit.

$453 \boxed{\div} \boxed{3} \boxed{=}$

Talk about what happens if the number does not divide exactly and there are numbers after the decimal point. Explain that this shows the answer is not a whole number.

A game to play

GUESS

This is a game for two players. One player enters a three-digit number into the calculator, such as 744. The other player tries to guess a number which will divide exactly into it, and the calculator is used to check the guess. One point is scored for each correct guess. The players then change over. The first player to score 10 points is the winner.

LINKS WITH THE ENVIRONMENT

Talk about division situations involving large numbers in everyday life.

- At school 156 children may be put in 6 house teams.
- On school journeys children often divide into smaller groups, each with a leader, or are allocated seats in 2s, 3s, 4s on buses and trains.

NOTES ON INVESTIGATIONS

Section A

Do the children realise that numbers which divide by 2 must be even? Do they then use the table of 3s to find even multiples of 3? Do any children multiply 2×3 and then use the pattern of 6?

Section B

Do the children come to realise that for divisibility by 9 the sum of the digits must be 9? For example, $27 \rightarrow 2 + 7 = 9$.

Do any children change the digits around? 126, 621, 162, 261, 612, 216.

Section C

Do the children use the link between multiplication and division when making up the clues? Do the children use word problems as clues?

Data 3

Purpose

- To introduce bar-line graphs

Materials

Squared paper, tape measure

Vocabulary

Data, bar-line graph, block graph, bar chart, most popular, questions, total, reach, longest, shortest, order, length, measure, least, most, twice, scales, fewer, more, altogether, different, number, amounts, squared paper, table

TEACHING POINTS

1 Graphs and scale

Remind the children how information, or data, can be shown on a block graph or bar chart. Build up a graph which shows, for example, favourite sports or pets. Talk about how a survey can be carried out and collect the information needed for the graph.

Remind the children about the need for a scale when drawing graphs in order to fit on all the information. Do the children understand the need to choose a suitable scale for this graph? The best scale will be the one most appropriate for the size of the paper they are using.

2 Bar-line graphs

Explain to the children that it is not always necessary to draw a block graph or bar chart. They can show the data equally well by just drawing a bar-line graph.

A group of children could throw an ordinary die 60 or more times and tally the number of times it shows each of the numbers.

Tally (or frequency) Total

	Tally	Total
1	II	
2	II	
3	⊞	
4	II	
5	III	
6	III	

From the results of the tally, or frequency scores, the children can draw a bar-line graph with the scores on the vertical axis.

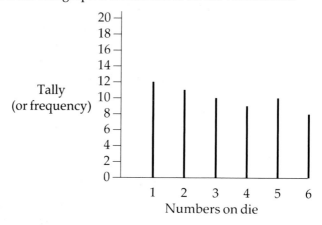

Ask some questions to help children use the information they have collected. Let them make up questions of their own.

3 From bar chart to bar-line graph

Draw a bar chart on the board. Ask the children to read the data and then redraw it themselves as a bar-line graph. This will help them to understand how the two graphs differ but show similar information.

4 Scales

The children will need practice in reading data from bar-line graphs using various scales; this will help them search for all the facts they need to interpret the information.
Let them show the same data themselves on two different graphs using different scales. Do they notice the effect of using different scales?

5 Horizontal bar-line graphs

Talk to the children about bar-line graphs that are horizontal. Build up an example of this with the children using span or cubit measurements and present the information as a horizontal line graph.

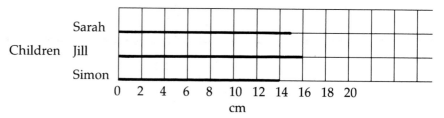

Do they see that the labels have changed places but the information is still there? Can they still interpret the graph drawn in this way?

A game to play

MAKE A GRAPH

Draw a large grid on the board. Let the children decide what the graph is about, for example marbles, and what the scale is. Divide the children into two groups. Let each group in turn suggest a number of marbles for the other group to show on a bar-line graph. One point is scored for each correct line. The game can be repeated using a grid with a different scale.

To extend the game, draw two grids of different scales; the groups have to draw the line correctly on both graphs to score a point.

6 Symbols for groups of units

Talk with the children about using a symbol to stand for a group of units. The symbol can be a box or a circle, almost anything in fact as long as the symbol won't be confused with an already understood symbol.

This is one example of a symbol representing a number when ⊕ represents 4 cars. Help the children to work out the total for each colour car in the chart. This could be as a result of a traffic survey or from finding the favourite colour of cars, and the children's own information can be displayed in a similar way. Do the children understand how to show 1, 2, and 3 cars as ◁, ◠ and ⊕.

		Total
red	⊕ ⊕ ◠	10
blue	⊕ ◠	6
white	⊕ ⊕ ⊕ ◁	13

Let the children suggest other symbols which can be used, such as ▭, □ and ●, to represent objects.

Talk about situations where parts of symbols may represent less than the group.

Number of play tickets bought by each class

Class 1   ▯ ▯ ▯ [

Class 2   ▯ ▯

Class 3   ▯ ▯ ▯ ▯

Class 4   ▯ ▯ ▯ ▯ [

▯   represents 10

[represents less than 10

7 Databases

Ask the children to find information about their heights, dates of birth, ages, etc. and draw a bar-line graph of the information. If a computer database is available they can enter and access information using it. A simple survey will give a purpose to the database and the children will often be able to display the information if a printer is attached to the computer.

8 Mental work

Talk with the children about the likelihood of events and decide whether they are very likely, likely, unlikely or very unlikely. For example,
'I will go to the football match tomorrow.'
'I will be a pop star one day.'
'I will be home at tea-time.'
  Children enjoy making up sentences like this, especially the very unlikely ones such as 'I shall turn into a monster with long teeth and red eyes tonight.'
  Turn the activity into a team game where each team has to make up sentences to match 'very likely', 'likely', 'unlikely' and 'very unlikely'. Each team member reads out a sentence and the other team guesses its degree of likelihood.

LINKS WITH THE ENVIRONMENT

Talk about everyday situations where we collect or use data.

- Traffic surveys
- Weather charts
- Growth charts of plants, animals, children
- Birds visiting a bird table
- Newspapers, advertising leaflets

NOTES ON INVESTIGATIONS

Section A

Do the children select various features of the buttons to use as data? For example, 4 holes, 2 holes, 0 holes. Do they draw a bar-line graph using a suitable scale for the paper provided?

Section B

Do the children collect information from other children by tallying or drawing objects? Do they draw two graphs using different scales but showing the same data? Do they understand that the graphs do not have to look the same to show the same data?

Section C

Do the children choose a number for Ann first? Do any children fix John's number first? Do they realise that John can have any number from 2 upwards? If he has 2, Paula has 0 crayons. Do they realise that John's number must be even since Ann has half? Do they draw two different bar-line graphs?

Purpose

- To practise division of money

Materials

Coins, calculator

Vocabulary

Share equally, between, cost, coins, equal amounts, numbers, sharing, divide, exactly, sold, half price, cheapest, most expensive, sale price, difference, different, money

TEACHING POINTS   **1 Sharing**

Talk to the children about how to share equally, using counters, bottle tops, crayons or other objects to make sure they understand the concept of equal. Talk about how coins cannot always be shared like this as the amount of money is not necessarily the same as the number of coins. Show examples where coins can't be shared into equal numbers:

can't be shared as and . The 10p coin needs to be changed down into 2p coins or 1p coins in order to be able to share equally.

Place different amounts on a table and ask children to share them into equal amounts of money.

This activity can be further reinforced by writing an amount on the board. One child can then use coins to share the amount equally between four friends, and write how much each one gets.

2 Recording division

Remind the children what the ÷ sign means and show them that they can record the division of money as they do numbers. For example, 80p ÷ 4 may be written as

$$
\begin{array}{r}
\text{p} \\
20 \\
\hline
4\,)\,80
\end{array}
$$

Children may of course devise their own algorithms for showing division of money.

Talk about how amounts may first be changed into pence or, alternatively left as pounds and pence.

$$
\begin{array}{r}
£ \\
\hline
2\,)\,1{\cdot}20
\end{array}
\qquad \text{changes to} \qquad
\begin{array}{r}
\text{p} \\
\hline
2\,)\,120
\end{array}
$$

Point out that when changing pence to pounds there must always be two digits in the pence. For example,

360p → £3·60   306p → £3·06

3 Shopping

Talk about shopping. Have the children ever seen this sign in the shops?

> Two for 40p

How can they find the cost of one item? It can be worked out using division and can be recorded like this:

$$
\begin{array}{r}
\text{p} \\
20 \\
\hline
2\,)\,40
\end{array}
\qquad \text{Each one would cost 20p.}
$$

Make up some shop prices and write cards for them.

> 3 for 15p   6 for 90p   4 for 60p

Let a child choose one card and ask another child to find the cost of one item.

A game to play

SNAP

Make out a set of cards showing various prices.

The rules are the same as ordinary SNAP. When matching cards turn up, 'Snap!' is called.

A harder variation might be to use only cards that show a number of items, such as

| 2 for 22p | 3 for 33p | 4 for £1 | 2 for 50p |

and call 'Snap!' when items of the same price for one turn up, for example

| 2 for 50p | and | 4 for £1 |

4 Half price

When do we see half price in shops? Why do shops have sales? Talk about stock-taking, selling old stock and closing-down sales. Do the children go shopping in the sales and what sort of things do they buy?

Make a simple wall shop with normal prices which divide exactly by 2. Do the children know how to find half of a price? Mark it as a $\frac{1}{2}$ price sale, and let the children ask one another questions about the new prices. A calculator might be useful here. You can extend the work by asking such questions as, 'How many of the notebooks at 30p each would I be able to buy if I had £1 to spend?' 'How much change is there?'

5 Cheap and expensive

Talk about what 'cheap' and 'expensive' mean. What are we comparing them with?
What they used to cost?
What other shops sell them at?
What they are made of?
Look in local shops and in catalogues.
Which item is the most expensive?
Which is the cheapest?
Which are the cheapest shops locally?

6 Mental work

Ask the children questions to work out mentally.
'What is half of 20p?'
'If 3 children share 60p, how much does each get?'
'Divide £1·40 by 2.'
'If 2 chocolate bars cost 50p, how much does one cost?'

USING THE CALCULATOR

Talk to the children about dividing amounts of money using the calculator. Remind them how to enter amounts so that £3·44 would be entered as 3·44.

Give them practice in showing pence as pounds and vice versa. Who can show it first?

Ask them to divide amounts such as £3·44 ÷ 4. Point out that if answers such as 5·322 appear on the calculator it means that the amount of money does not divide exactly. Ask them to find, for example, the cost of one calculator if six cost £18·60.

LINKS WITH THE ENVIRONMENT

Talk about everyday situations involving money.

- Shops. Talk about where shopping is cheapest. What sort of shops are most expensive? A local survey might be interesting. Talk about the price of items in a jeweller's window. What sort of shops are quite cheap? Which are the cheapest sweets? Compare prices of household goods in cheaper and dearer shops. Talk about famous shops such as Harrods in London.
- Shop sales. Talk about the January sales. Why January? What is meant by a bargain? When are other popular times for sales?
- Catalogues. Look at and compare prices in catalogues. Find out, for example, the cost of a set of calculators for the class.
- Shopping. Where do we see '3 for 20p' etc.?
- Compare today's prices with those that parents or grandparents can remember.

NOTES ON INVESTIGATIONS

Section A

How do the children approach the problem? Do they use pencil and paper, coins or the calculator? Do they record the division accurately? Do they share £1·20 into equal amounts each time? Do they change the £1·20 into coins that will share equally? For example, 50p, 10p and 50p, 10p   or   20p, 20p and 20p, 20p and 20p, 20p.

If they use a calculator and work in pounds and pence, do they realise that any more than two digits after the point indicates that the amount does not divide exactly? Do they find a range of possibilities such as 2 × 60p, 3 × 40p, 4 × 30p, 5 × 24p, 6 × 20p, 8 × 15p, 10 × 12p, 20 × 6p, 30 × 4p, 120 × 1p?

Section B

Do the children use coins to divide into equal amounts? Do they realise that if a number will divide by 6 it will also divide by 3 and 2, and that if a number will divide by 4 it will also divide by 2? Do they realise that they can make another number that will divide exactly by doubling the £1·80? Do any children just try to divide each of the amounts by 2, 3, 4, 5, and 6 using a trial and error method? Do any use a calculator and appreciate that the display can show whether the number divides exactly nor not?

Section C

Do the children set the cheapest price first and then set the other prices? For example,

Cheapest	£1	× 2 (2 for £2·00)
'Middle'	£1·02	× 2 (2 for £2·04)
Dearest	£1·05	× 3 (3 for £3·15)

Number 15

Purpose

- To introduce eighths of shapes and numbers
- To introduce the equivalences of halves, quarters and eighths

Materials

Paper circles, paper squares, squared paper

Vocabulary

Equal, fraction, circle, square, fraction wall, half, quarter, eighth, whole, equal parts, different, missing, fraction sentence

TEACHING POINTS   **1 Eighths**

Talk with the children about eighths. Cut, or explain how to cut, a cake or chocolate bar into 8 equal pieces by first cutting it into halves, then quarters, then eighths. Talk about how to write $\frac{1}{8}$ and what it means: 1 out of 8 equal parts.

2 Eighths of shapes

Ask the children to fold a rectangle of paper into halves, then quarters, and then eighths. Talk about some of the ways that this can be done.

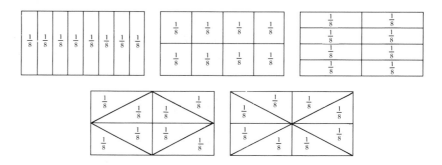

Label each part $\frac{1}{8}$

Point out that to be eighths the fractions must be equal.

Mark a rectangle as '1' or '1 whole' on one side and into $\frac{1}{8}$'s on the other. Ask how many eighths there are in 1 whole. Talk about the equivalence and that $\frac{8}{8} = 1$.

This folding activity can be repeated with the octagon. The circle and square are referred to in the pupils' books.

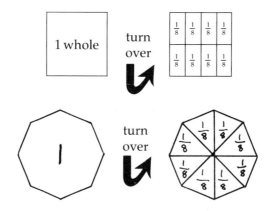

An interesting and decorative mobile can be made from all the different shapes.

3 Equivalence of $\frac{1}{2}$, $\frac{1}{4}$, $\frac{1}{8}$

Draw a fraction wall on the board or ask the children to make one using strips of paper. This is sometimes called an equivalence board or chart.

1			
$\frac{1}{2}$		$\frac{1}{2}$	
$\frac{1}{4}$	$\frac{1}{4}$	$\frac{1}{4}$	$\frac{1}{4}$
$\frac{1}{8}$ $\frac{1}{8}$	$\frac{1}{8}$ $\frac{1}{8}$	$\frac{1}{8}$ $\frac{1}{8}$	$\frac{1}{8}$ $\frac{1}{8}$

The fraction wall can be used to provide imagery for children's understanding of equivalence. Take this in stages, each time talking about ways of recording fractions and asking questions related to them.

- $\frac{2}{2} = 1$ $\frac{4}{4} = 1$ $\frac{8}{8} = 1$
  'How many $\frac{1}{2}$s in 1?'
  'How many $\frac{1}{8}$s in 1?'

- $\frac{2}{4} = \frac{1}{2}$ $\frac{4}{8} = \frac{1}{2}$
  'How many $\frac{1}{4}$s in $\frac{1}{2}$?'
  'How many $\frac{1}{8}$s in $\frac{1}{2}$?'

- $\frac{2}{8} = \frac{1}{4}$ $\frac{6}{8} = \frac{3}{4}$
  'How many $\frac{1}{8}$s in $\frac{3}{4}$?'

4 Eighths of numbers

Talk with the children about eighths of numbers. Draw 8 circles. Ask the children to colour $\frac{1}{8}$ red, $\frac{3}{8}$ blue, $\frac{2}{8}$ green. Can they say what fraction is left?

An alternative is to put out eight coloured counters when $\frac{1}{2}$ must be red, $\frac{1}{4}$ blue and $\frac{2}{8}$ green.

This work could be extended to other multiples of 8 such as 16 and 24.

5 Further equivalence of $\frac{1}{2}$, $\frac{1}{4}$, $\frac{1}{8}$

Ask the children to draw shapes and divide them into eighths, then colour $\frac{1}{2}$ red, $\frac{1}{4}$ blue, $\frac{1}{8}$ green. What fraction is not coloured?

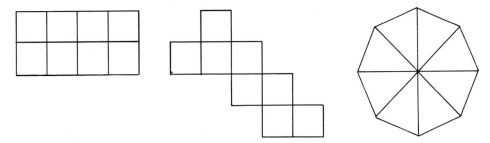

Some interesting mathematical art work can be developed by extending this to other multiples of 8 such as 16 or 24.

6 A game to play

FRACTION DOMINOES

This is a game for 2, 3 or 4 players. Make a set of fraction dominoes like these, using $\frac{1}{2}, \frac{1}{4}, \frac{3}{4}, \frac{1}{8}, \frac{2}{8}, \frac{4}{8}$ etc. A further set of cards with the fractions written in words could also be added. The game is played like dominoes, with each player in turn trying to match an end piece with one of their dominoes.

7 Mental work

After some practice with practical activities, ask the children to work out fractions mentally.

- $\frac{1}{2}$ of 2, 4, 6, 8, 10, . . . , 20
- $\frac{1}{4}$ of 4, 8, 12, 16, 20
- $\frac{3}{4}$ of 4, 8, 12
- $\frac{1}{8}$ of 8, 16, 24

Extend children by asking more difficult problems such as $\frac{3}{8}$ of 16, etc. Use simple word problems like 'What is $\frac{1}{8}$ of 8 sweets?'

USING THE CALCULATOR

- Revise how to find $\frac{1}{2}$ and $\frac{1}{4}$ of numbers using the calculator.
- Show the children how to find $\frac{1}{8}$ of numbers. For example, 'To find $\frac{1}{8}$ of 16 we divide by 8.' Enter

Choose the numbers carefully to avoid decimals when dividing.

LINKS WITH THE ENVIRONMENT

Talk about everyday situations involving $\frac{1}{8}$.
- Sharing cake, pizza, chocolate, sweets.
- Look for eighths in window patterns.
- Felt tip pens and crayons often come in packets of 8.
- Some biscuit and cake boxes are divided into eighths.
- Sharing money out between 8 children.

NOTES ON INVESTIGATIONS

Section A

Do the children find several different ways to fold the square into eighths?

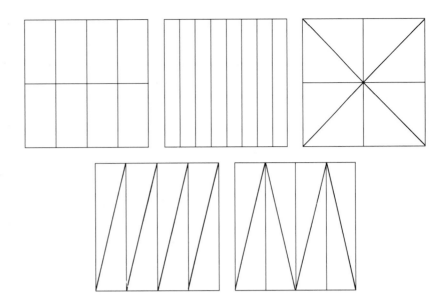

Section B

Do the children colour and label the fractions correctly? Do they find alternative ways to colour the same fractions? Do they realise that $\frac{1}{2}$ of 24 = 12, $\frac{1}{4}$ of 24 = 6, $\frac{1}{8}$ of 24 = 3?

Section C

Are the children systematic in finding fractions of 40?

$\frac{1}{8}$ of 40 = 5
$\frac{2}{8}$ of 40 = 10
$\frac{3}{8}$ of 40 = 15 etc.

Do they realise that the numbers are part of the 5 times table?
    Similarly do they realise when finding eighths of 32, the numbers are part of the 4 times table?

Length 3

Purpose

- To introduce the notation for m and cm, 1 m 27 cm → 1·27 m
- To give practice in the addition and subtraction of m and cm
- To give practice in measuring

Materials

Height measurer (if available), long tape measure, ruler, trundle wheel, metre stick, tape measure

Vocabulary

Metre, centimetre, long, high, height, tall, taller, wide, wider, longer, reach, shorter, twice, half, measurements, difference, length, distance, measure, trundle wheel, metre stick, tape measure, nearest metre, equal, total

TEACHING POINTS

1 Centimetres

Give the children some revision practice in estimating and measuring in cm. Remind them that we should always write 'cm' and not 'cms'.

2 The metre stick

Show the children a metre stick. Ask them how many centimetres there are in 1 metre. Talk about the things in the room that are about 1 metre long. Do the same for $\frac{1}{2}$ metre.

3 Writing cm as m

Talk about how longer distances should be measured in metres rather than centimetres, because of the large numbers that would otherwise be needed.

Measure and cut strips of card with the lengths written on in cm.

| 26 cm | 15 cm | 8 cm |

Ask a child to hold the metre stick and another child to hold one of the cards next to it, and say how many cm there are altogether.

| 1 metre | 26 cm |

In metres and centimetres this is 1 m 26 cm; explain how it can be written in metres as 1·26 m.

Give the children plenty of practice in changing cm into m. Make sure that the children understand the relationship between cm and metres. Stress particularly that 1 m 8 cm is written as 1·08 m. Talk about writing lengths like 26 cm as 0·26 m.

4 Measuring in m and cm

Give the children practice in measuring distances accurately using the long tape, for example, 1·53 m or 153 cm.

5 Measuring heights of people

Talk about how we measure people's height – the children need to know their heights for the work in section A. If a wall height measuring device is available, show them how to use it. If not, a long tape measure can be stuck to a wall with the low numbers at the bottom so the heights are read correctly. Let the children write their heights and change them from cm to m.

6 Using reference books

Children find it interesting to discover some facts of their own about animal measurements. For example, how far would the longest snake stretch in the classroom or playground? The *Guiness Book of Records* is especially useful. These activities will lead naturally to addition and subtraction. For example, how much longer is a crocodile than a grass snake?

7 Addition

Show the children how to set down the addition of m and cm. Stress how important it is to line up the points, and then the addition is the same process as for HTU.

$$
\begin{array}{r}
\text{m} \\
2{\cdot}67 \\
+\ 1{\cdot}24 \\
\hline
\end{array}
$$

8 Subtraction

Talk about finding the difference in measurements, such as when comparing the heights of two people or the lengths of two animals. Again, stress the importance of setting down the subtraction carefully; point out that the working is done in the same way as HTU subtraction.

$$
\begin{array}{r}
\text{m} \\
3{\cdot}54 \\
-\ 1{\cdot}38 \\
\hline
\end{array}
$$

9 Measuring long distances

Talk with the children about various measuring instruments and their advantages and disadvantages.
- Trundle wheel. It's quick but children have to remember to count the clicks for metres. Also it cannot go right up to walls so the result is often approximate.
- Metre stick. This is an accurate measure. But remind children that it needs to be laid end to end, possibly using chalk marks to count how many metres.

- Long tape measure. This is easy to use if nothing is in the way to prevent it from being stretched out. It is accurate because it measures in metres and centimetres.

Give the children practice in measuring longer distances using these instruments.

10 Estimating

Estimating is an important skill and plenty of practice is essential. This might be done in a fun way. For example:
'A badger is 95 cm long. Would a badger fit on your desk?'
'Find out the length of a crocodile. Mark the approximate length in chalk on the floor.'

Games to play

BRING ME . . .

This can be played in small groups. Have a metre stick, tape measure or cards of different length as a guide for estimating. Ask the group to find an object of a certain length, for example 50 cm. It is then measured and a point is scored for a reasonable estimate.

Alternatively, the children can mark their estimate on the floor with chalk or pieces of string.

CHANGING

Call out 136 cm. A point is given to the first member of a team to write 1·36 m on the board.

A variation is to play a snap or domino type game where cards

showing, for example, $\boxed{136\ cm}$ or $\boxed{1\cdot36\ m}$ are matched

HOP, SKIP OR JUMP

Ask the children to do a hop, a skip or a jump to estimate length. For example, from a starting point, hop for 3 metres. Allow other children to measure and check the distances hopped by their friends to see how close they were to 3 metres.

11 Mental work

Change cm to m and m to cm mentally. Let the children write distances such as 154 cm or 168 cm in metres from oral instructions.

USING THE CALCULATOR   The children can practise addition and subtraction on the calculator by entering heights and lengths correctly. 2·67 m is entered as $\boxed{2·67}$. Let the children use their calculators to work out questions related to distances, such as
'How much taller is Ann than Harjit?'.
The first to get the correct answer may ask the next question.

LINKS WITH THE ENVIRONMENT   Talk with the children about measuring lengths or distances in everyday situations:

- Reading the speedometer on a bike or car. These usually measure in miles or kilometres
- Heights of people. Why do we need to know heights?
- Talk about sizes of clothes, buying knitting or sewing patterns to make them.
- Who is the tallest person in the country? What problems do very tall or very short people have?
- How do we know how tall people in history were? Discuss finding skeletons and how antique objects can give us clues as to the size of people they were designed for.
- Sizes of animals. Discuss the biggest and the smallest. Are the biggest animals necessarily the fiercest? Talk about planning zoos so that animals have comfortable spaces to live in.
- Sport. What are the world records for high jump, long jump and pole vault?

NOTES ON INVESTIGATIONS   ### Section A

How do the children find their friend's reach? Do they write it in cm or m?

How do they approach the investigation? Do they write the measurements and add them until they get close to 3·05 m? Or do they mark 3·05 m on the wall with chalk, using a long tape measure and then ask their friends to mark off their reaches along it?

Section B

Do the children understand the instructions? Do they choose a sensible body length to allow them to easily resolve the other parts of the animal? Do they also realise that they have to choose a body size, initially, that will ensure the final animal fits on the paper?

Section C

Do the children find their own height first in m and cm? Do they then use a calculator to multiply their height by 130?

Weight 3

Purpose

- To introduce the kg, g notation: 1234 g = 1·234 kg
- Addition and subtraction of kg and g
- To give practice in weighing

Materials

Balance scales, bathroom scales, materials to make parcels, rubber bands, cup-hooks, paper, collection of weights

Vocabulary

Kilogram, gram, weight, heaviest, lightest, difference, weigh, weighing, scales, stretches

TEACHING POINTS

1 Writing g as kg

Show the children some weights, both g and kg. Talk about how we write them. Ask how many grams there are in a kilogram. Show them how we write it as 1 kg = 1·000 kg.

Talk about how we write weights which are greater than 1 kg. For example, 1500 g = 1·500 kg.

Write a weight on the board such as 1200 g. Ask two children to find the weights that make this amount. Put signs on the board like this.

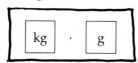

Ask the children to separate the weights and stand holding them in the correct position under each sign.

Give the children practice in changing g to kg.

2 The kilogram

Talk about weights which may be much heavier than a kilogram:

- potatoes at the greengrocers
- parcels at Christmas or birthdays
- mail order deliveries
- buying rabbit food
- the children's own weights
- furniture in the home or classroom

Show the children how we write, for example, $1\frac{1}{2}$ kg as 1·500 kg, $5\frac{1}{2}$ kg as 5·500 kg, and why we do this.

3 Addition of weight

Ask the children to think of times when people add weights together.

- Weight lifters put extra weights on the bar and give the total weight.
- Suitcases are weighed at an airport and then weights are added together so that the amount of fuel needed for the flight can be calculated. Talk about why each passenger is given a maximum weight of luggage.

Show the children how to set down addition of kg and g:

```
  kg
  2·446
+ 3·245
  ─────
```

Remind the children that the digits to the right of the point are grams, although we don't put a g sign. Explain that when adding the numbers we do it in the same way as ThHTU addition and that it is very important to keep the digits lined up correctly in the columns.

4 Addition activities

Give the children practical experiences in weighing things in the classroom and then finding the total weights using kg notation.

5 Subtraction of weight

Talk about how there might be times when we want to find the difference in weight between two things.

- working out weight loss when people are dieting
- working out the weight gains of a young baby
- comparing the difference in weights of prepacked or package foods at the grocers
- buying 'help yourself' foods such as muesli, flour or nuts and adding more to make up the weight needed

Show the children how to find the difference by subtracting, explaining that the process is the same as for subtraction of ThHTU.

kg
6·474
− 2·162
‾‾‾‾‾

6 Subtraction activity

Give the children two or three books to weigh together. Remove one book and ask the children to do a subtraction to find the weight of the missing book.

7 Games to play

FIND THE SIGN

Hang a ⃞ kg sign at one side of the room and a ⃞ g at the other. Write a weight on the board, for example, 1432 g. Write each number on a piece of paper, ⃞1 ⃞4 ⃞3 ⃞2 , and give one to each of four children. Ask them to stand under the appropriate sign in the right order:

WEIGHT PAIRS

Make about 12 pairs of cards like these:

| 1540 g | 1·540 kg |

Shuffle them and lay them face down. Each player takes turns to turn two cards over. If they turn over a matching pair they keep them. If not they leave them face down in the middle and shuffle them around again. The winner is the player who collects the most pairs.

8 Mental work

Ask the children to write g as kg and vice versa from oral instructions.
   Let the children practise changing weights in kg and $\frac{1}{2}$ kg into grams.

Ask the children to add weights such as 1 kg and 500 g as a word problem. For example:
'Two parcels weigh 1 kg and 500 g. What is the total weight?'

USING THE CALCULATOR   Call out a number of grams and let the children show it in kg on the display, for example, 1642 g as 1·642.
Ask them to show kg as grams, such as $2\frac{1}{2}$ kg as 2500.

LINKS WITH THE ENVIRONMENT   Talk about everyday situations which involve weight. These might include:

- Shopping activities and adding amounts of shopping
- Check ins at airports
- Olympic Games, weight lifters
- Finding animal weights
- Sending parcels by post
- Weighing pick'n'mix sweets

NOTES ON INVESTIGATIONS   **Section A**

Do the children make realistic choices to make up the parcel weights? Does it appear that they are developing their ability to estimate weights greater than 1 kg?

Section B

Are the children beginning to develop the ability to estimate weight? Do they make realistic judgements about the difference in the weight of objects? Do they use scales to check their estimates? If the weight difference is very far out, do they learn from their mistake and judge better next time?

Section C

Do the children experiment in order to mark the scale? Do they realise that there is not necessarily the same amount of 'stretch' for the same amount of weight added, and that the scale needs to be carefully graduated? Do they use their home-made scale to work out the weight of other objects? Do they make good judgements when weighing other objects?

Volume

Purpose

- To find the volume of shapes by counting cubes

Materials

Centimetre cubes, squared paper, glue

Vocabulary

Shapes, centimetre cubes, volume, greater, cuboids, more, squared paper, layers, cubic centimetres, larger, different size

TEACHING POINTS

1 Using cubes to measure volume

The volume of something is the amount of space it fills. Talk with the children about this, and how we can measure volume using cubes.

Show the children an open box and ask them how they could find out how much it will hold. What can be used for filling it – sand, reels, marbles or cubes, perhaps? Groups of children could try filling the box in different ways. Encourage them to realise the problem with using something that can't be counted. Let them work out which objects fill the box best.

'Are reels good for filling the box? Are there any gaps?'
'What happens when the box is filled with cubes?'
'Which is the best shape for filling the box? Why?'

Explain how we can record the volume of a box, for example, volume = ☐ cubes. Can the children work out other ways, perhaps pictorially?

Give the children practice in filling boxes with cubes and recording the volume. The boxes should be carefully chosen or made so that the cubes fit exactly.

2 Estimation

Show the children some different sized boxes. Ask them to estimate how many cubes each will hold and to place them in order of volume. This can be checked by filling the boxes with cubes. Again, the boxes should be carefully chosen.

3 Conservation activities

Show the children some different sizes of cube, including the cm cube. Explain that centimetre cubes are so named because the edges measure 1 cm. The children check this with a ruler. These are the cubes that are used for measuring.

Develop the concept of conservation by giving 20 cubes each to two children and asking them to build different shapes. Talk about the ways of recording this such as volume = 20 cubes. Talk about the volume of both the shapes and how although they look different, the volume is the same because both were made with 20 cubes.

Remind the children what a cuboid is; this is referred to in the pupils' book.

A game to play

TWO THE SAME

Play the game in two groups. One group builds three shapes from cubes. Two of the shapes must have the same volume but look different.

The second group has 10 seconds to look at them all and say which two of the shapes have the same volume. One point is given for each accurate estimation.

LINKS WITH THE ENVIRONMENT

Talk about everyday situations where we see boxes being filled with solid shapes.

- At the supermarket – smaller boxes or cartons are packed in large containers.
- At home – Oxo cubes, bathcubes, and some sweets, such as fudge cubes, pack in larger boxes
- At school – mathematics equipment; stacks of PE blocks or building blocks.

NOTES ON INVESTIGATIONS

Section A

Do the children make cuboids? Do they find all the possibilities, i.e. 12 × 1 × 1, 6 × 2 × 1, 4 × 3 × 1, 3 × 2 × 2? Do they understand why the volume of all their cuboids is the same?

Do they make different cuboids with 15 cubes in the same way?

Section B

Do the children build a cuboid each time? Do they adopt a system for finding all the possibilities for the base of the cuboid?

$1 \times 1 \times 24$

$1 \times 2 \times 12$

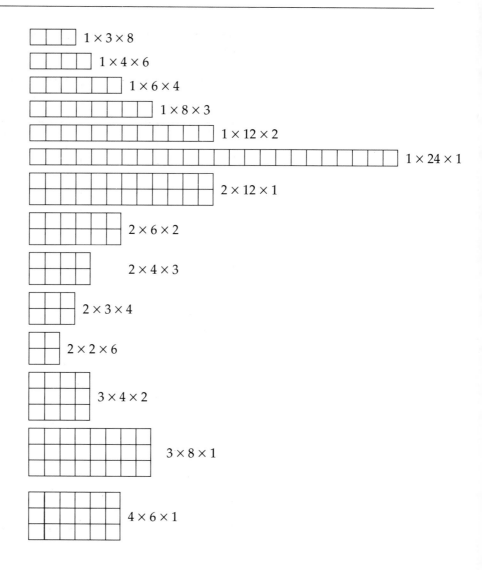

$1 \times 3 \times 8$

$1 \times 4 \times 6$

$1 \times 6 \times 4$

$1 \times 8 \times 3$

$1 \times 12 \times 2$

$1 \times 24 \times 1$

$2 \times 12 \times 1$

$2 \times 6 \times 2$

$2 \times 4 \times 3$

$2 \times 3 \times 4$

$2 \times 2 \times 6$

$3 \times 4 \times 2$

$3 \times 8 \times 1$

$4 \times 6 \times 1$

Section C

Do the children have difficulty in making shapes with holes in? Do they see a pattern in their answers?

volume of shape	volume of hole
8	1
10	2
12	3
14	4
16	5

As an extension for this investigation, use squared paper as a base for the shapes.

base	hole	grid size	
8	1	3 × 3	
10	2	3 × 4	
12	3	3 × 5	
14	4	3 × 6	

Time 3

Purpose

- To introduce the number of days in the months
- To write the date in words and numbers
- To revise the use of the calendar

Materials

Squared paper, year calendar (a month by month calendar would be useful as well), clock stamp for month clock

Vocabulary

Calendar, names of days of the week, names of months of the year, New Year's Day, date, leap year, month clock, year, oldest, youngest, birthday, date of birth, year calendar

TEACHING POINTS

1 Days of the week

Talk with the children about the days of the week. Make up a selection of questions and turn it into a quiz.
'How many days are in a week?'
'What day is it today?'
'What day was it yesterday?'
'What day will it be tomorrow?'
'What day will it be in 3 days' time?'
'Which days are schooldays?'
'Which days make up the weekend?'
'Which is the first day of the week?'
'How many days in a fortnight?'
   Make a class chart showing the days of the week.

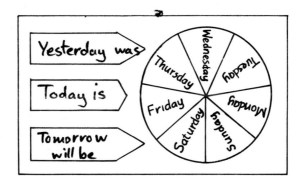

   Ask the children to use the chart to write the days of the week in order starting with a different day each time.

2 Months of the year

Talk with the children about the months of the year. Make up another quiz to help children think of the sequence of months.
'How many months are there in a year?'
'Which month are we in now?'
'What was last month?'
'What will next month be?'
'Which month is Christmas in?'
'What month is after the Christmas month?'

A game to play

MONTHS

Write the name of one month on each of 12 pieces of paper. Give them out to 12 children at random. Ask the children to stand in month order. See how quickly different groups can sort themselves into the right order. Start the year with different months and not necessarily January.

The game could be adapted to order the days of the week.

3 Calendars and seasons

Talk about the way we record time in calendars and diaries. Collect some calendars showing months and years. Explain that we divide up the year into four seasons called spring, summer, autumn, winter. Talk about the seasons and what we associate with each one. Which months make up each season?

Show or draw a calendar for any month and ask questions such as: 'How many Fridays are there?'
'What day is the 17th?'

4 Introduce the number of days in the months

Explain that some months have 30 days, some have 31 days and February has 28 days and 29 in a leap year.

Show the children the knuckle method for finding the number of days in a month.

Ask them to use it to find the number of days in particular months. The traditional rhyme is a good way of remembering how many days in each month.

30 days has September,
April, June and November.
All the rest have 31
Except February alone
Which has 28 days clear
And 29 in each leap year.

5 Leap year

Talk about a leap year and how it occurs every four years. Can the children find out how and when the leap year came about?

Early mathematicians studied star formations and calculated that there were 360 days in a year. This is thought to be the reason for using 360° in a circle. Later the year was calculated to be $365\frac{1}{4}$ days and so every 4 years an extra day was added in order to 'catch up'.

Explain that for a leap year the year number divides exactly by 4. Use a calculator to show that leap years are 1988, 1992 etc.

Talk about the customs of leap year. Mention that the Olympic Games are held every leap year.

Does anybody have a birthday on February 29th? How is this celebrated in other years?

6 Time facts

Ask the children to write some time facts. Write them on a chart and display them in the classroom.

> *Time facts*
>
> 7 days in 1 week
> 2 weeks in 1 fortnight
> 52 weeks in 1 year
> 12 months in one year
> 365 days in 1 year
> 366 days in 1 leap year
> 4 seasons – Spring, Summer,
>   Autumn, Winter

7 Writing the date in words

Talk with the children about how we record time by the date. Explain that we can write the date in words, for example, 'Thursday, 8 June 1989'. A class date chart could be made which the children take turns to change.

Write the date on the board every day and ask the children to copy it before starting their work.

8 Writing the date in numbers

Talk with the children about writing the date using numbers only, such as 8.6.89.

Draw a clock face and show the months.

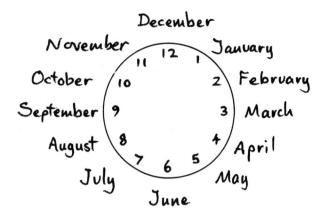

Explain that because January is the first month of the year we can write it as 1, February as 2, March as 3, etc. Also because the first two digits of the year number only change every 100 years, we often just show the last two digits. Therefore 8 June 1989 becomes 8.6.89. Explain that some people write it 8/6/89.

Ask the children questions to reinforce this idea.
'Which is the 9th month?'
'Which is the 5th month?'
'Which month of the year is August?'

Put some dates in words on the board, and give the children opportunities to write the date in numbers and vice versa.

9 Activities

- Keep personal diaries or class diaries, perhaps for a week or month.
- Keep a simple weather chart showing both the date and the weather.
- Make a graph of birthday months, and discuss this.
- Measure newly planted cress or mustard seeds to record their daily growth.

10 Mental work

Ask the children questions about

- the days of the week, months of the year or date and time facts
- the number of days or complete weeks holiday from school
- the number of days in the first four months of the year

USING THE CALCULATOR   A calculator may be used to help the children in their mental work, for example, in adding the days in four consecutive months of the year or working out whether 1992 or 1994 is a leap year.

LINKS WITH THE ENVIRONMENT

Talk with the children about everyday situations involving days, dates, months, year.

- borrowing public library books for 3 or 4 weeks
- sporting events – the Olympic Games held every four years; other regular sporting events, for example Wimbledon tennis or the F.A. cup for football
- TV programmes – school broadcast dates
- holidays and special times of year
- history – study of how the names of the days and months originated and how time has been recorded in the past
- birthdates in school – what is the range of the dates in the class?

NOTES ON INVESTIGATIONS

Section A

Do the children record the date and year correctly in words or numbers? Do they state the reason why the dates are important to them – for example, 'The date I was born'?

The children's dates could lead to discussion and further investigation.

Section B

Do the children have difficulty in putting some of the dates of birth in order? Do they write the dates using words or numbers? Are their questions sensible? Do their questions show that they understand the date when it is written in numbers only?

Section C

Are the children's questions clear? Do they find the answer to their questions before asking a friend to do the problem?

Angles 3

Purpose

- To recognise acute and obtuse angles
- To recognise straight angles
- To revise 45°, 90° and introduce 180°
- To make comparisons with right angles

Materials

Folded paper right angle

Vocabulary

Acute, obtuse, right angle, straight angle, degrees, folded, different, size, 45°, 90°, 180°

TEACHING POINTS

1 Right angles

Do the children remember what a right angle is? Remind them that it measures 90°. Can they show one with their arms?

Ask them to fold a right angle from a piece of paper. Can they see any other right angles in the classroom?

2 Half right angles

Let the children fold a $\frac{1}{2}$ right angle from their paper right angle. Ask how many degrees are in a $\frac{1}{2}$ right angle.

3 Acute angles

Use a large piece of cardboard and make an angle pointer with 2 right angles marked on it.

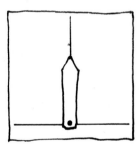 

Use the angle pointer to show children that if they make any angle less than a right angle then it is called an acute angle. Let the children take turns to show acute angles on the pointer.

A fun way to show an acute angle is to draw a crocodile's mouth with the acute angle between the jaws.

These are some other ways to show acute angles.

Can the children find acute angles in the classroom? Can they make acute angles in PE with their legs or arms?

4 Obtuse angles

Use the angle pointer to show children that angles greater than 1 right angle and less than 2 right angles are called obtuse angles.

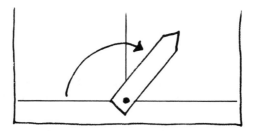

What do the children notice about the angle on the other side of the pointer?

Show obtuse angles in different ways as for the acute angle using scissors, rulers and other objects.

Can the children find any obtuse angles in the room?

5 Straight angle

Use the angle pointer to show the children what a straight angle is, i.e. it goes across from A to B.

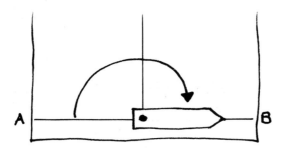

Do they realise that a straight angle is also two right angles, so it must measure 180°? Can they see any straight angles in the classroom?

Ask them to open a book to show an acute, an obtuse and a straight angle.

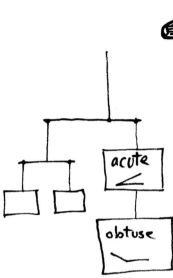

6 Naming angles

Ask the children to write the names of the angles and draw them on cards. Hang them up as mobiles.

Games to play

ARMS

Ask a child to stand at the front of the class and make angles with his or her arms. The rest of the children have to write down the name of the angle or, alternatively, hold up a card showing the type of angle.

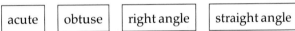

| acute | obtuse | right angle | straight angle |

This could also be played with a teacher calling 90°, 45°, 150°, 60°, etc. and the children making a reasonable estimate of the angle size.

ANGLE TRAIL

Let the children draw an angle 'trail'. Then other children follow a partner's trail, marking in acute, obtuse and right angles wherever possible:

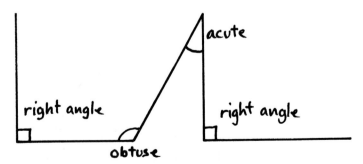

LINKS WITH THE ENVIRONMENT

- Buildings. Look for acute, obtuse and straight angles in buildings. Talk about architects and draughtsmen, and ask what would happen if they got the angles wrong.
- Art and craft. Look at pattern work in art and angles in model making.

- Clocks. Look at the hands of a clock to see the different angles made.
- PE. Make angles with arms and legs. Look at large climbing apparatus.

NOTES ON INVESTIGATIONS

Section A

Do the children understand acute, obtuse and straight angles? Do they show several different examples of all three types?

Section B

Do the children realise that each sector is 45°? Do they make a folded $\frac{1}{2}$ right angle to help with the drawing? Do they colour the correct number of degrees? Do they draw different colour combinations to make up 90°?

Section C

Do the children structure their drawings to show 1, 2, 3, . . . 45° angles? Do they think of all possibilities? 45°, 90°, 135°, 180°, 225°, 270°, 315°, 360°.

Module 5 Pupils' book 1
RECORD SHEET

Class . . . .   Pupil . . . .

Topic	*Section*			*Assessment*	*Comment*
Number 1	A	B	C		
Number 2	A	B	C		
Shape 1	A	B	C		
Number 3	A	B	C		
Area 1	A	B	C		
Number 4	A	B	C		
Data 1	A	B	C		
Money 1	A	B	C		
Number 5	A	B	C		
Length 1	A	B	C		
Weight 1	A	B	C		
Capacity 1	A	B	C		
Time 1	A	B	C		
Angles 1	A	B	C		
Number 6	A	B	C		
Number 7	A	B	C		
Shape 2	A	B	C		
Number 8	A	B	C		
Area 2	A	B	C		
Number 9	A	B	C		

General comments:

Module 5 Pupils' book 2
RECORD SHEET

Class .... Pupil ....

Topic	Section			Assessment	Comment
Data 2	A	B	C	☐	
Money 2	A	B	C	☐	
Number 10	A	B	C	☐	
Length 2	A	B	C	☐	
Weight 2	A	B	C	☐	
Capacity 2	A	B	C	☐	
Time 2	A	B	C	☐	
Number 11	A	B	C	☐	
Angles 2	A	B	C	☐	
Number 12	A	B	C	☐	
Shape 3	A	B	C	☐	
Number 13	A	B	C	☐	
Area 3	A	B	C	☐	
Number 14	A	B	C	☐	
Data 3	A	B	C	☐	
Money 3	A	B	C	☐	
Number 15	A	B	C	☐	
Length 3	A	B	C	☐	
Weight 3	A	B	C	☐	
Volume	A	B	C	☐	
Time 3	A	B	C	☐	
Angles 3	A	B	C	☐	

General comments

MATERIALS REQUIRED FOR MODULE 5 ▬▬▬

balance scales
bathroom scales
beaker
bottles (including 250
  ml, 750 ml, 1 litre)
boxes for opening out
  to make nets
boxes of different
  shapes for display
calculators
calendars (year,
  month-by-month)
card
centimetre cubes
clock faces
clock stamps
clothes
coins
compass
containers (less than
  25 ml in capacity)
counters
crayons
cubes
cup

cup-hook
dice
felt tip pens
funnel
glue
height measurer
ice-cream tub (large)
long tape measure
map of Britain
map of the world
measuring jugs (100
  ml, 500 ml, 1 litre)
metre stick
mirrors (double-sided)
mug
multiplication square
number cards
number line
100 square
pack of children's
  playing cards
paper circles
paper fastener
paper squares
parcel-making
  materials

plane shapes (squares,
  circles, equilateral
  triangles, hexagons,
  pentagons)
rubber bands
rulers
scissors
soft toys
squared paper (1 cm, 2 cm)
sticky tape
string
structural apparatus
tape measures
templates (equilateral
  triangles, squares,
  etc.)
tracing paper
transparent grid sheets
trundle wheel
weights (up to 1 kg)
water
yogurt pot

GLOSSARY FOR MODULE 5

acute angle	An angle between 0° and 90°.
algorithm	An algorithm is a method or a procedure for finding a solution. For example, decomposition is an algorithm for subtraction.
a.m.	Ante meridiem. The time before midday.
angle	An angle is the amount of turn or rotation. Angles are measured in degrees with 360° in a whole turn.
anti-clockwise	*See* clockwise.
approximate	A number or measurement which is not exact but is accepted as being close enough.
area	Area is the size or amount of a surface, and is usually written in units of square measurement.
balance	A balance is a set of scales.
bar-line graph	A form of graph where the data is represented by lines.

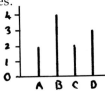

bilateral symmetry	*See* symmetry.
block graph	A block graph is a form of pictorial representation where the data is represented by columns.
capacity	The capacity of a container is the amount that it will hold.
Carroll diagram	A form of diagram for classifying data devised by Lewis Carroll, author of *Alice in Wonderland*. Here is an example.

	red	not red
circle	● ●	○
not a circle	■	◻

Celsius	A temperature scale where 0 °C is the freezing point of water and 100 °C is the boiling point.
centimetre	$\frac{1}{100}$ of a metre (abbreviation: cm).
circle	A circle is a set of points, all of which are a fixed distance (the radius) from a fixed point (the centre).

clockwise	This is the direction in which the hands of a clock turn. Anti-clockwise is the opposite direction.
column	A column is a list of numbers (or letters) or squares in a grid going down a page.
commutative	An operation for example, $(+, -)$ is commutative if numbers can be used with it in any order and still give the same answer. Addition is commutative, since, for example, $3 + 1 = 1 + 3$. Multiplication is commutative, since, for example, $3 \times 2 = 2 \times 3$. Subtraction is **not** commutative, since $3 - 1 \neq 1 - 3$. Division is **not** commutative, since $4 \div 2 \neq 2 \div 4$
compass	An instrument for showing direction. The four points of the compass are N, S, E, W. The eight points of the compass are N, S, E, W, NW, NE, SE, SW.
conservation	Remaining unchanged even though the position or situation changes. For example, a litre of water is always a litre of water irrespective of the shape of its container.
constant function	The use of the constant function on a calculator allows numbers to increase or decrease by a fixed amount. For example, the numbers 2, 5, 8, 11, . . . are increasing by the constant $+ 3$.
co-ordinates	An ordered pair of numbers, for example (4, 5), to show a point on a graph or grid.

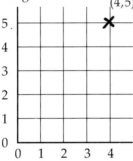

cube	A cube is a solid with all its six faces square and all its edges equal in length. For example, a die is a cube.
cuboid	A cuboid is a solid with six faces that are all rectangles. Opposite faces are the same.
data	Data is information or facts which have been collected. It is often displayed as a block graph, or bar chart.
decomposition	Decomposition is a method for subtraction where, for example, a 'ten' is changed into ten units.

$$
\begin{array}{r}
5\,{}^{1}2\,{}^{1}4 \\
-\ 3\ \ 1\ \ 7 \\
\hline
2\ \ 0\ \ 7 \\
\end{array}
$$

degrees	Angles are measured in degrees. There are $360°$ in a full turn.

digit	A digit is a single figure or symbol in a number system. For example, the digits in 347 are 3, 4 and 7.
edge	An edge is the line formed when two faces of a solid meet.

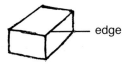

equilateral triangle	An equilateral triangle is a triangle with all three sides the same length.
equivalent fractions	Fractions are equivalent if they can represent the same fraction. For example, $\frac{1}{2}, \frac{2}{4}, \frac{3}{6}, \frac{4}{8}, \frac{5}{10}, \frac{6}{12}$ are equivalent.
estimate	To estimate is to make an approximate judgement of a number, amount, etc. without measuring it.
face	A face is the flat side of a solid shape.
factor	A factor is a number which divides exactly into another number. For example, 3 is a factor of 12.
fraction	A number less than 1, written as $\frac{a}{b}$ where a is the numerator and b is the denominator.
gram	A gram is a unit of weight. It is $\frac{1}{1000}$ of a kilogram. The abbreviation for gram is g.
graph	A graph is a picture or diagram to make information more easily understood. Data is often shown by picture graphs, block graphs or bar charts.
grid	A set of intersecting parallel lines, usually at right angles to one another and the same distance apart.
grouping	Put into sets with an equal number in each.
half square method	The half square method for finding an area is the process of counting a $\frac{1}{2}$ square or more than a $\frac{1}{2}$ square as a whole square, and ignoring anything less than a $\frac{1}{2}$ square.
hexagon	A hexagon is a plane shape with six sides. A regular hexagon has all its sides equal in length and all its angles the same size.
hexagonal prism	A prism with end faces that are hexagons.
hexominoes	Sets of six squares joined together by their edges. Here are two.

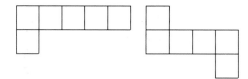

horizontal	A line is horizontal when it is parallel to the Earth's horizon. It is at right angles to a vertical line.

intersect	To cross.
irregular shape	A shape that is not regular. All of its sides and angles are not equal.
kilogram	A kilogram is the standard unit of weight (abbreviation: kg). A kilogram is equal to 1000 grams.
kilometre	1000 metres (abbreviation: km)
line of symmetry	A line of symmetry on a shape divides the shape into halves so that one half is a mirror image of the other.
litre	A litre is a unit of capacity (abbreviation: l, not to be confused with 1). One litre is a little over $1\frac{3}{4}$ pints.
magic square	A magic square has numbers on a square grid such that each row, column and diagonal add up to the same total. This is a 3×3 magic square.

2	7	6
9	5	1
4	3	8

measure	To measure is to find a size or quantity by comparison with a fixed unit.
metre	A metre is the standard unit of length (abbreviation: m).
millilitre	$\frac{1}{1000}$ of a litre (abbreviation: ml).
minute	A minute is 60 seconds.
multiple	Multiples of a number are given by that number multiplied by whole numbers. The multiples of 4 are 4, 8, 12, 16, . . . The multiples of 10 are 10, 20, 30, 40, . . .
multiplication square	A multiplication square is a square which shows the multiplication table.

×	1	2	3
1	1	2	3
2	2	4	6
3	3	6	9

negative number	A number less than zero. For example, -1 is one less than zero.
net	A two-dimensional shape that can be folded to make a three-dimensional shape. For example, is a net for a cube.

notation	The way in which symbols are used to represent, for example, quantities. The notation for a length of seven centimetres is 7 cm.
number bond	A number bond is a relationship between a set of numbers. The following are examples of number bonds: $3 + 4 = 7$, $9 - 1 = 8$, $2 \times 5 = 10$, $12 \div 2 = 6$.
number sentence	A number sentence is a mathematical statement or sentence, for example, $2 + 1 = 3$.
obtuse angle	An angle between 90° and 180°.
palindrome	A number that reads the same forwards as backwards. For example, 99, 525.
parallelogram	A four-sided shape with opposite sides equal and parallel.
pattern	A pattern is an arrangement of numbers, etc. according to a rule. A pattern allows us to predict what might come next. For example, in the sequence 1, 2, 3, –, –, 6, the missing numbers are 4, 5, since the pattern is adding one each time.
pentagon	A pentagon is a five-sided plane shape. A regular pentagon has all its sides equal in length and all its angles the same size.
pentominoes	Sets of five squares joined together by their edges.
perimeter	The distance all the way round a closed shape.
place value	Place value is the value of a symbol or digit in a number system due to its position. For example, in the number 22, each 2 has a different value because of its position.
plane of symmetry	A three-dimensional shape may possess a plane of symmetry where one half of the shape is a reflection of the other. For example
plane shape	A plane shape is a two-dimensional shape. For example, circles and triangles are plane shapes.
p.m.	Post meridiem. The time after midday.
pound (weight)	An imperial unit of weight. A pound is a little less then half a kilogram.
prism	A prism is a solid with the same shape along its length, so that it has uniform cross-section. This is a triangular prism.
pyramid	A pyramid is a solid shape with a polygon for its base. The other faces are triangles which meet at a vertex called the apex.

quadrant	A fourth part. When drawing a graph the first quadrant is as shown:

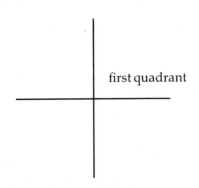

first quadrant

reach	A person's reach is the length from finger tip to finger tip when the arms are extended sideways.
rectangle	A rectangle is a four-sided shape with four right-angles and opposite sides equal in length.
regular shape	A regular shape has all its sides the same length and all its angles the same size, for example, a square.
relationship	A connection between numbers or quantities.
right-angle	A right-angle is a quarter of a complete turn. It is measured as an angle of 90°.
rotate	To turn.
rounding	Writing a number to a required level of accuracy. 126 is written as 130 when rounded (up) to the nearest 10. 124 is written as 120 when rounded (down) to the nearest 10.
row	A row is a list of numbers or letters across the page.
scale	One distance is represented by another distance. For example, 1 cm : 1 m or 1 centimetre represents 1 metre.
sequence	A set of numbers written in order according to a relationship.
solid	A solid is a three-dimensional shape, for example, a cube.
square	A square has four equal sides and four right-angles.
square corner	A square corner is a right-angle.
standard unit	Standard units are generally accepted units. A standard unit for measuring length is the metre. A standard unit for measuring weight is the kilogram.
straight angle	180°.
stride 	A stride is a long step measured by the distance from heel to heel or toe to toe.

structural apparatus   Structural apparatus is apparatus to show how the number system works.

symbol   A sign that represents a number or a letter.

symmetry   Line symmetry is the exact matching parts on either side of a straight line. This is sometimes called bilateral or mirror symmetry.

template   A template is an object or shape to draw around.

tessellate   A shape or shapes repeat to form a pattern without gaps or overlaps.

tetrahedron   A solid shape with four triangular faces.

triangle   A triangle is a plane shape with three straight sides.

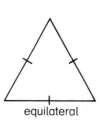  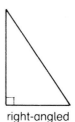 

equilateral   isosceles   right-angled   scalene

triangular prism   A triangular prism is a prism whose end faces are triangles.

vertex (plural vertices)   The vertex is a point where lines or edges meet.

vertical   At right angles to the horizontal.

vertices   See vertex.

volume   The volume of a solid is the amount of space it occupies. The units of measurement are usually cubic centimetres or cubic metres.

weight   The weight of an object depends on the gravitational force acting on it. An object on the Moon will weigh less than on Earth although its mass will remain the same.